WOMEN
IN
CLASS STRUGGLE

by
Marlene Dixon

SYNTHESIS PUBLICATIONS
San Francisco

Published by Synthesis Publications, P.O. Box 40099 San Francisco, California 94140.

Women in Class Struggle is an anthology of articles originally published in the journal *Synthesis* (now entitled *Contemporary Marxism*).

ISBN 0-89935-000-3 Copyright (c) 1978 by Synthesis Publications.
Expanded Edition (c) 1980.

Printed in the USA. 5th Printing.

Trade distribution:
U.S. and International: Synthesis Publications
U.S. only: Carrier Pigeon, 75 Kneeland St., Boston, MA 02111
New York City: Delhi Distributors, 1181 Amsterdam Ave., N.Y., NY 10027

CONTENTS

*Includes "Women: The Oppressed and Exploited Majority," from the Provisional Program of the Democratic Workers Party for the 1980's.

Note

The author wishes to express her profound opposition to the broad right-wing attack currently being waged against the rights of women. This attack is most viciously aimed at the right of women to control their own bodies. The result has been the denial of abortion on demand to hundreds of thousands of women across the country. We strongly oppose this attack on working class women.

In light of the move by the right-wing against the rights of women, the author wishes to state clearly her support for the passage of the Equal Rights Amendment.

M.D.

Introduction

by Betita Martínez

This book is an expression of experience, study and analysis going back many years, a process that included the women's movement of the late 1960's and early 1970's in which Marlene Dixon played a leading role. She drew numerous lessons from that experience, which are described in this book. One of the most important was that the autonomous (separate) women's movement—because it segregated women politically—had failed to defeat the sexism rampant in the "New Left." Stubborn left-wing male sexism remained a barrier to organizing women as a significant part of the New Left, to moving the women's movement toward Marxism, and to an understanding of sexism in terms of class relations. As Marlene Dixon writes in the present book:

> The prolonged existence of the autonomous movement, with its penchant for psychological theorizing, made it difficult to see that the defeat of sexism and racism *in the left* was an *organizational*, not attitudinal, problem. The solution to the prevalence of both sexism and racism must be found in the process of party formation itself. The very structure of a revolutionary party must provide an organizational basis upon which equality between comrades can be developed and enforced.

Guided by these convictions, Marlene Dixon joined together with other women in building a party—today, the Democratic Workers Party, whose founding was formally

i

announced November 6, 1979. The relationship between being women and the kind of party they sought to build was clearly described by Marlene that day in November:

> ... we women are the exploited *majority*, in all countries, of all races and cultures, in different degrees exploited, to be sure, but exploited one and all. Not by men, but today by a system of capitalism (and what does it matter that our subjugation preceded capitalism). Today it *is* capitalism that lies at the root of our subjugation, that lies at the root of the general subjugation, the general despair, alienation, call it what you will—that the capitalist system produces and reproduces, not only in America but all over the globe. The truth is that capitalism exploits and oppresses not only women and minorities, but globally, the vast majority of humanity.
>
> As working class women we wanted to build a party of the majority, which is the working class—for *only* in this way could we fight back against *all* injustice. As women we *must* fight all injustice because ours is the universal, the fundamental, image and reality of inequality and exploitation—to end ours, *all* inequality and exploitation must be abolished. To accomplish that demands the abolition of classes, and to abolish classes, to achieve social equality, we must abolish the *root* of inequality, and that requires the abolition of capitalism, not only as a national economy, but also as a global world economy.
>
> We, as women and as children of the working class, wanted to build a party that would unite men and women, white, black, brown, asian, native and immigrant: we wanted to build a party that not only "believed in" equality, but *practiced* it—for as women we were tired of being second-class citizens—in fact, we were sick and tired of anyone being a second-class citizen!
>
> As women, we also knew we had to have a party that recognized the real role of women in the leadership of the party, and that such a recognition *had* to rest in the successful combat against racism, sexism, nationalism, any form of class relations—that is to say, exploitative relations. That conviction, and the struggle to realize it, is integral

to the nature and structure of the party, to its style of work and its worldview. We are not bourgeois feminists, but we *are* proletarian feminists, and we believe, and we hope you will too, that we have brought unique and powerful new visions to the struggle for working class liberation.

For some time, we did not make public the leadership of the party and this was for two reasons. First, we did not want stars and myths, or images, or hot shots or celebrities to carry the party or portray its nature, as the mass media have so often caused to happen. Secondly, we wanted to show, in practice, by deeds, just what women could do—for who knows better than we what it is to be invisible? The barriers of sex prejudice are real: Who listens to women? Who respects women? Who believes women can fight for the whole class? In the face of the stone wall of so-called "left sexism," we knew we had to demonstrate our party, our ability to organize it; to show in practice, as it says in the song "Bread and Roses," that "the rising of the women is the rising of the class." We believe that, and it is true, and we've demonstrated it to be true. *Now* we are men and women, we are white, brown, black, asian; *now* we are, but only because we struggled for that unity and still struggle for it. Yet every ounce of energy and hope we put into forging the sexual and racial unity of the party has been essential to our whole vision, for such unity *must* be the beginning, must shape the struggle of the 80's and of the future beyond the 80's.

That vision and an immediate program for the struggle are contained in the Provisional Program of the Democratic Workers Party, adopted in September, 1980. We present here the section from the program on *Women: the Oppressed and Exploited Majority.*

Women: The Oppressed and Exploited Majority

(Text prepared by Nancy Cooke and Elizabeth Doerr, Program Committee)

Against the narrow self-serving feminism of the bourgeois feminists and the male bigotry of many organizations of the left, the Democratic Workers Party, men and women alike, stands for proletarian feminism. Proletarian feminism stands for the recognition of the essential *human* social equality of women in our society. As proletarian feminists not only must we fight for the recognition of the humanity of women; we must also fight to build a new society, a working class socialist society, in which women have an equal hand.

As proletarian feminists we understand that we must not put off the struggle for the emancipation of women until we are engaged in socialist construction. The struggle for the rights of women must be waged now. We understand that both sexism and racism are the brutal anti-human products of capital which must be smashed. Therefore, the fight for the full, real human equality of women must be one of our highest priorities. To engage this struggle we need a new women's movement, a proletarian feminist movement, that will fight not just for legal equality, but for the real *social* human equality of all women. As proletarian feminists we understand that to fight for the rights of working class women is to fight for the rights, as women, of all women. For working class women are the most oppressed and exploited members of our society—in fact, superexploited—and the majority of women are working class.

> This superexploitation is expressed by: 1) the denial by capital of compensation for labor consumed in production and reproduction of labor power; 2) the systematic undervaluation of waged female labor; 3) forcing women disproportionately into the worst and most degrading jobs; and 4) forcing women into part-time or full-time work in addition to full responsibility for domestic labor (thus married, or single parent, working women hold down two full-time jobs, but are paid wages for only one).

> Upon investigation, working class women are clearly the most oppressed, superexploited sector of the entire proletariat. The greatest burdens are carried by racial and national minority women."

> Marlene Dixon, *Women in Class Struggle.**

Today austerity capitalism has intensified the super-

---

*Quotes throughout this section are from *Women in Class Struggle* by Marlene Dixon.

exploitation of women in working class families. Austerity and inflation are driving women increasingly into the labor force. At the same time, no services are provided to counteract the loss of the mother from the home. Thus the working class women in the labor force must work two full-time jobs, one waged, one unwaged—while simultaneously being forced into the worst jobs at the lowest wages.

Clearly all advances made by the workers' movement which serve the interests of the working class as a whole will also serve working class women. In fact it is the duty and the obligation of the labor movement to fight for the rights of working women. Yet this leaves an enormous realm of women's life and oppression and suffering untouched.

Likewise, although we have seen the most remarkable upsurge of women throughout the world in the last two decades, in the United States we have seen the largest segment of this movement become totally absorbed into the questionable pursuit of the Equal Rights Amendment. This movement we call bourgeois feminism, for in reality it fights only to gain juridical and legalistic equality with men under the rule of capital. This means bourgeois and petty bourgeois women will become equal to the men of their class. Bourgeois women can become controllers of banks and finance capital, petty bourgeois women can become vice presidential lieutenants.

For 10 years this has been the obsession of the bourgeois feminist movement, under the hegemony of such CIA types as Gloria Steinem (who admitted collaborating with the CIA for years as director of a research group covertly funded by the CIA), while the lives of working class women remain virtually untouched. For 10 years the bourgeois feminists have been content to channel the entire struggle of women into a struggle for juridical equality. And yet during those same years that the bourgeois feminists have marched down the narrow ERA path, the conditions of life of all women have been under increasing attack.

The right wing has managed not only to thwart the passage of the ERA; it has also managed to mount a well-financed vicious attack against the right of women, most especially working class women and permanently unemployed women, to control their own bodies, an attack which has gone virtually unopposed. At the same time there has been an astronomical increase in the number of forcible rapes and rape/murders. The incidence of reported wife beating is now over 1 million annually. Child abuse has become a national phenomenon. Forced sterilization is systematically inflicted on minority women. Sadistic pornography has become a multi-billion dollar industry until today we live in a culture which makes millions of dollars in profits from propaganda that glorifies the mutilation and torture of females.

Will the Equal Rights Amendment stop the cruel and exploitative social relations of capitalism? Will the ERA stop death from illegal abortions, wife/murder, rape/murder, wife beating, forced sterilization and child abuse? Will juridical equality in any way alleviate the massive cruelty and degradation of females in our society? Can genuine equality be legislated in a country whose Supreme Court has just declared that it is legal to deny funding for abortions to poor women?

Nonetheless, it is not the Equal Rights Amendment as a piece of legislation in itself that we are criticizing, but rather the reduction of the greater part of the women's movement to the passage of a piece of legislation. In the end we must support ERA, with all its faults, because it has come under such virulent attack by the neo-fascist right wing.

Just as we oppose the bourgeois feminist movement, so too we strongly denounce the organizations of the left which liquidate the oppression and exploitation of women into the class question and ask all women to wait until some future heaven on earth before they struggle for their social equality and the recognition of their humanity. In the face of the rise of acts of violence and sadism against women; in the face of the rise of the right wing attack against the reproductive rights of women and legal rights of women; in the face of the massive discrimination, exploitation and oppression of working class women in our society, we can see that it is nothing but the most self-serving unreconstructed petty bourgeois male bigotry to turn a deaf ear to the plight of one half of the human species.

> The conflict between men and women, husbands and wives, is not some "petty bourgeois feminist plot" to divide the working class, but a real product of the cruel and exploitative social relations of capitalism. In fact, no sphere of a working class woman's life is free from exploitation facilitated by institutionalized male supremacy.
>
> Marlene Dixon, op. cit.

As proletarian feminists we call for the right of all women to control their own bodies. This means the freedom to control their own powers of reproduction, their own sexuality; this means freedom from the abuse of rape, wife beating, and victimization by sadistic pornography.

Everywhere in the world where the process of socialist construction is occurring, women do have the right to control their own bodies in almost every sphere. Birth control and abortion are a woman's right under socialism. Rape is a disappearing crime under socialism. Cultural sadism against women which incites violence against women is outlawed in socialist countries. It is for all of these reasons we say that to be a genuine proletarian feminist one must also be a proletarian socialist. Sexism is the product of the cruel and exploitative social relations of capitalism and women shall never be freed from exploitation and oppression until we are all freed from the domination of capital over every aspect of our lives.

PROGRAM FOR CHANGE

The Right of All Women
To Control Their Own Bodies

Reproductive Rights

> Women's reproductive capacities are supervised by the state because capital needs to regulate population, to control production of the product, children.
> Marlene Dixon, op. cit.

The Democratic Workers Party is committed to the right of all women to control their own bodies. This right includes the right to bear children and the right to choose not to bear children. The state does not have the right to control a woman's body as it sees fit simply because she was born female. To advocate the right of a woman to control her own body is in no way anti-child. We believe that every woman has the right to decide whether or not she wishes to give birth. We are not animals in the field; we are freely choosing human beings.

The Right To Abortion

The Supreme Court granted the right to abortion on demand in 1973, at a time when an estimated 1 million women each year had to seek abortions illegally, facing infection, lack of anesthesia and lethal techniques. Prior to 1973, at least 350,000 were admitted to hospitals each year for complications from such abortions; from 500 to 1000 died. And what was the fate of the woman who did not have the money to pay the back alley abortionist or to fly to Sweden? For the desperate woman faced with an unwanted pregnancy and determined not to go under, the only choice was self-abortion—through knitting needles, umbrella ribs, coat hangers, turpentine, kerosene, castor oil, soap solutions or other chemicals which can lead to mutilation and death.

It is this torture, the torture of the living, to which the current right-wing attack on abortion rights would condemn millions of working class women, particularly those permanently unemployed and on welfare. Middle class women can still pay their gynecologist $1,000 for the privilege of abortion or $200 to an abortion clinic, while poor and working women are denied abortions through the recent federal legislation restricting Medicaid funds to pay for them. Abortion for women on public assistance becomes the issue upon which the hatred of women, the hatred of the working class, and racism converge.

The right wing is now calling for a Human Life Amendment to the U.S. Constitution. This amendment, adopted as a plank by the Republican Party in their 1980 election platform, would give the rights of personhood to a fertilized egg. Passage of the amendment could result in women who choose to have an abortion being tried for first-degree murder!

1. We oppose the denial of abortion to any woman; we oppose any legislation or restriction of abortion rights which condemns women to the illegal abortionist, to the risk of mutilation and death. The right of all women to reproductive freedom must be guaranteed through adequate and available federal, state and local funding for abortion, childbirth and pregnancy-related care.

2. We oppose the Human Life Amendment and the thrust of legislation denying women the right to choose to have an abortion under any circumstances.

The Right to Birth Control

Because of women's biological role as childbearer, the availability of safe and effective birth control is crucial to their participation in society. Birth control currently available is not safe and effective. Twenty deaths per 100,000 users per year result from oral contraceptives, and both IUD and pill users face an increased risk of hospitalization. The pharmaceutical industry, to keep profits high, refuses to research and produce more effective and safe methods.

1. We call for funding of publicly supervised research into safe and effective birth control financed by the drug companies which make millions of dollars in profits selling unsafe birth control. Male as well as female birth control measures should be developed. Once new methods are developed they should be provided free on demand. Barriers should be removed to birth control services for all teenagers who request them.

An End to Sterilization Abuse

One of the most insidious forms of imposed population control is sterilization abuse. By 1968, 35.3% of the women of reproductive age in Puerto Rico had been sterilized; today almost 20% of Native American women have been sterilized. The sterilization program is financed by the government through the Department of Health, Education and Welfare. A 1972 study found that doctors suggested sterilization 6% of the time to private patients, and 77% of the time to welfare patients.

In addition, millions of young women are rendered involuntarily sterile because of the epidemic of pelvic infections caused not only by venereal disease but also by IUD's, an epidemic virtually ignored by health authorities because of their contempt for the reproductive rights of women.

1. We do not condemn sterilization in itself. We condemn it when it is manipulated and forced. We oppose involuntary sterilization and call for regulations to be enforced requiring that sterilization be truly voluntary, informed and competent. Spousal consent should not be required.

2. There should be universal and detailed educational programs on birth control, sterilization, abortion, and reproductive illness.

Sexual Rights

A Woman Has the Right
To Be Sexually Self-Determining

A woman's enforced dependency and her consequent subjugation is further justified in the social definition of woman as primarily a sexual object, whose principal reason for existence is in passively giving her body for male sexual satisfaction and in the bearing of his children.

Marlene Dixon, op. cit.

As proletarian feminists who stand in opposition to the subjugation of women and who reject any notion of women as primarily sexual objects for the gratification of others, we strongly affirm the right of women to have control over their own sexuality, as an aspect of the right to control their own bodies.

We believe in the possibility of and the necessity for non-exploitative enduring relationships between men and women that are based upon equality and mutual respect. A woman is not the property of her husband any more than he is her property. A woman has the right to refuse to be raped by her husband. We believe that a woman should not be governed by "double standards" that are designed to maintain women as the property of men, while leaving men to do as they please.

We also believe in the right of all human beings to have sexual relationships with whatever individuals they choose, and affirm the right of an individual to their own sexual preference. We are against discrimination against homosexuals and lesbians on the basis of their sexual preference; we oppose all the formulations of anti-homosexual legislation now abounding. We think an individual should not be defined or judged as a human being on the basis of sexual preference.

Against Abuse That Violates
A Woman's Body and Liberty

We stand adamantly opposed to all forms of torture, terror and abuse against women which violate a woman's physical integrity and liberty as a human being.

A woman is raped every 8 minutes in the United States; one out of every ten female murder victims in the U.S. is killed during rape or other sexual offenses; up to 20% of all hospital emergency room visits by women have been attributed to wife beating; pornography which subjects women to dramatized rapings, stabbings, burnings, beatings, gaggings, bindings, tortures, dismemberments, mutilations and deaths is a $4,000,000,000 a year industry in the United States alone.

The widespread and growing practices of rape, rape/murder, wife beating and cultural incitement to female abuse (sadistic pornography) constitute a massive attack against women in our society. In response to such terrorism, torture and abuse, we call not only for specific social programs to combat these brutal and sadistic crimes against women; we also call for the right of women to be armed in order to defend themselves and we call for the most severe and swift punishment of the perpetrators.

> Rape is an expression of aggression and hatred
> vented upon a social inferior; it is an act of spiritual
> murder even when it is not accompanied by murder
> in fact.
>
> Marlene Dixon, op. cit.

Forcible rape is one of the most common and fastest
growing violent crimes in the U.S. today. From 1970 to 1975
the number of rapes reported increased by 48%. Estimates
place the number of rapes annually at 200,000. One out of
every four women in the U.S. will experience rape or
attempted rape in the course of her lifetime. According to
the San Francisco Police Department's Sex Crimes Division,
there are fewer "clean" rapes and more rapes in which women
are brutalized, blatantly humiliated and tortured, as well as
sexually assaulted.

> Rape is a social punishment and an affirmation of
> male superiority and female bestiality, buttressed
> by the bourgeois morality's "animal" image of
> woman, the Madonna-Whore, as one who secretly
> "enjoys" her degradation and humiliation in the act
> of forcible rape.
>
> Marlene Dixon, op. cit.

Rape is always an act of humiliation and degradation; it is
an act of aggression. This is why when one man wants to
humiliate another man, he will participate in or himself rape
another man. One of the largest areas of rape completely
ignored in the general literature is the rape of men by
men—as in the schools with young boys, in the Army, in the
prisons and under other circumstances. In some ways the
situation of men is even more hopeless than that of women
because men are even less likely to raise the issue or protest
the act when it occurs.

Historically the response of law enforcement agencies and
medical personnel to the female victims of rape has been
nothing but a perpetuation of the humiliation and degradation
inflicted by the rapist. Thus the woman is "twice-victimized"
because of the mythologies of male bigotry which maintain
that self-avowed rape victims have "asked for it," and that
furthermore "no woman can be raped against her will." Thus
rape is the only crime where the victim becomes the accused.

Furthermore, if a woman is determined enough to press

for prosecution of her attacker, after being subjected to contemptuous and voyeuristic interrogation, the likelihood of getting a conviction is about 10%. The courtroom becomes an inquisition and the victim is put on trial.

Finally, women who have defended themselves, that is, women who have killed their assailants in self-defense have been viewed as murderesses by the criminal justice system. This means that the right to self-defense accorded to all owners of private property is denied to females with respect to their own bodies!

The human atrocity known as rape is perpetrated on such a massive scale that the lives of all women, in one way or another, are affected by its occurrence. The victims become a lesson to all would-be victims: that women in our society are prey and must thereby physically restrict their movements. It is the epitome of bourgeois relations between men and women that women must go out alone in the world or walk at night at their own risk. Women are portrayed as hysterical if they calculate and compute who among the men they pass are hunters, stalking them. If women are carefree and fearless, then they are considered fair game not only by the rapist but also by the police and courts. It is the product of the decadence of our society that half of the human race lives under the threat of this form of indiscriminate terrorism.

As proletarian feminists we denounce rape as the physical form of male hatred and aggression toward women. So long as forcible rape is a growing crime, women are quite literally not free to control their own bodies. Therefore, we call for:

1. The right of women to defend themselves against physical assault and rape by men. This includes training in the art of self-defense as part of the physical education provided by public schools for female children and adolescents and the provision of publically funded classes for adults.

Women should be allowed to arm themselves in order to defend themselves. Murder in self-defense should be justifiable homicide when women are defending themselves from rape.

Women should not have to rely upon an unresponsive criminal justice system in order to deter rapists.

2. Law enforcement, legal and medical personnel should be trained in dealing with rape victims and should accord rape victims the due process, compassion and support to which they are entitled.

3. Every effort should be made to apprehend, try and

convict proven rapists. Convicted rapists should be incarcerated for a long time.

We deplore the virulent racism of the criminal justice system. We strongly oppose the discriminatory sentencing of black rapists as opposed to white rapists. We think that all rapists should be punished regardless of color and without racist discrimination. The vast majority of instances of rape are intra-racial, that is, black men raping black women and white men raping white women.

We strongly disagree with those organizations of the left which maintain that to call for increased prosecution of rapists is racist because it would only put more black men in jail. First of all, most rapists are white men; therefore, calling for increased prosecution means increased prosecution of white men. Secondly, most black male rapists rape black women; black women have the right to have their assailants punished and incarcerated. The vast majority of men are NOT rapists; the vast of majority of black men are not rapists. Only a small minority of men of any race are rapists, and those men should be locked up so they can't rape anyone. To deny to all women, white and black, protection from rapists because the criminal justice system is racist is to put the interests of a small minority of rapists above the interests of all women.

Finally, the white ruling class has used rape laws, like all laws, to unjustly imprison national and racial minority men, and in particular black men (Scottsboro Case). To conclude from this that rapists should go free, to prey upon all women, is to ask all women of all races and nationalities to suffer terrorism and risk murder because of a racist system of justice. This total disregard for the plight of women on the part of certain segments of the left simply feeds the reactionary bourgeois feminists' ideology that all men are the enemy, that Marxism and class analysis are irrelevant to the condition of women, that the left has no concern for the eradication of rape.

We strongly disagree with the bourgeois feminists who fail to see rape and the brutality against women in our society as the product of class relations between men and women under capitalism. The failure to deal with the subjugation of women as a product of capitalism leaves them helpless to posit any solutions other than to hate all men and to strive without hope of success to combat the ideology of male supremacy. Because they do not deal with the material basis of the oppression and exploitation of women in Marxist terms, they become extreme in their condemnation of all men as the enemy and are without any vision of a future where men and women can live and work together without brutality and exploitation. Their failure to transcend a bourgeois feminism is the direct product of the class interests of the vast majority of narrow feminists who do not strive for the abolition of capitalism, but only an equal share in the spoils.

Wife Beating

> Bourgeois sexual morality reflects property relations in so far as it defines a woman's body, the children produced from her body and her labor power as the private property of the husband or protector.
>
> Marlene Dixon, op. cit.

There are approximately 1.8 million instances of wives who are beaten by their husbands annually. A Kansas police department study found that in 85% of the cases of domestic homicide, the police had been called at least once before the murder took place, and in 50% of the cases, they had been called five times or more before the homocide occurred. These appalling statistics reflect the fact that a woman is considered the property of her husband, to do with as he pleases. Domestic troubles are considered a man's private affair. Often working class women stay, despite repeated beatings, because they are financially dependent upon their husbands, because they are afraid of losing their children, and because there is no place for them to go. When a woman does have the courage to press charges, few judges do more than caution the man or give him a suspended sentence. This only spells more danger for the wife, who then has to contend with an enraged wife beater who retaliates against her for reporting him to protect herself. This *vicious* circle can and does often go on for years.

1. We call for the reform of the criminal justice system to allow a wife to have her husband convicted of battery.

2. When a man engages in wife beating, custody of the children should automatically go to the wife if she so chooses.

3. Shelters should be established for battered women with public funding. To stop wife beating, there must be shelters provided where working class women can escape from their husbands.

Against Cultural Incitement to
Violence Against Women (Sadistic Pornography)

> Against the image of the "pure and virtuous asexual woman" is the dark counter-image of woman as victim, of a creature whose slow and bloody torturing to death is a source of sexual satisfaction and pleasure.
>
> Marlene Dixon, op. cit.

Under advanced monoply capitalism we live in a decadent society, a society where rape is the all-American crime, where sadistic violence and sexual enslavement are not remote phenomena but visible at your local record shop, where 1.5 million children annually are used in commercial sex (prostitution or pornography). Pornography has become a multi-million dollar industry in the U.S. and has become increasingly "hardcore," culminating in *Snuff*, billed as a movie which recorded the actual murder, rape and mutilation of the actress. At the same time there is mounting evidence on the linkage of sadistic pornography to actual rape. Against no other group in society could handbooks or blueprints for sadistic violence, mutilation and torture be made available with such safety and impunity.

We think that sadistic pornography should be outlawed. We do not agree with those who state that it violates freedom of speech to demand the outlawing of images of torture and sexual sadism. It is not within the spirit of the First Amendment, written to ensure political rights and freedom, to use "freedom of expression" against the actual freedom and physical safety of women.

1. We oppose the sale of images of women being bound, raped, tortured and murdered for sexual stimulation. Sadistic pornography should be outlawed.

Social Equality and the ERA

Nowhere is the right wing's virulent opposition to the rights of women clearer than in its campaign against the Equal Rights Amendment, an amendment which states simply that "Equality under the law shall not be denied or abridged because of sex." As Phyllis Schlafly, head of STOP ERA, put it, a vote against ERA is a vote against everything the women's movement stands for. The ERA faces defeat due to the organized opposition of right-wing forces, including the Ku Klux Klan, John Birch Society, Daughters of the American

Revolution and the Mormon Church. The 1980 Republican Convention voted overwhelmingly not to endorse the Amendment.

1. In light of this right-wing attack, we support passage of the Equal Rights Amendment. At the same time, we call for those labor laws which offer real protection to women not to be abolished, but extended to both men and women.

OUR VISION FOR THE FUTURE

Our Party stands for a socialist society in which sexism can cease to exist because its foundation—capital's exploitation of man by man and of woman by man—ceases to exist. No longer will there be a need to justify the exploitation of half of the human race on the basis of capital's ideology of male supremacy. No longer will there be an economic basis for the superexploitation of female labor power or the ideology of male supremacy.

We recognize that even if we change the mode of production from capitalism to socialism, it will still be a long struggle to combat male bigotry. However, it will be immediately possible to outlaw all institutionalized discrimination. Measures will be taken to compensate for past deprivation and victimization. Socialism can provide the social and economic substructure upon which a united working class can successfully wage a vigorous struggle against the prejudices and hatreds left over from the era of capitalism.

The Provisional Program of the Democratic Workers Party for the 1980's contains:

Introduction: The Challenge of Transnational Capital; the U.S. Working Class; Women: the Oppressed and Exploited Majority; Racial and National Minorities; The Rights of Working Parents; Youth; Age; Taxation; Political Repression and Civil Liberties; Criminal Justice and Prisons; Education; Health; Housing; Environment; Religion and Socialism; and War and Peace. The *Provisional Program* is available from Synthesis Publications, P.O. Box 40099, San Francisco, California 94140. $1.00.

THE CENTRALITY OF WOMEN IN CLASS STRUGGLE

On the Super-Exploitation of Women

Wages for Housework and Strategies of
    Revolutionary Fantasy

The Subjugation of Women Under Capitalism:
    The Bourgeois Morality

Left-Wing Anti-Feminism: *A Revisionist Disorder*

Monopoly Capitalism and the Women's Movement:
    Against the Socialist Feminist Response to
    Harry Braverman's *Labor and Monopoly Capital*

On the Super-Exploitation

of Women

Feminism and Marxism, Marxist Feminism, all have floundered in one way or another on the shoals of the dual problems of biology and the family. The self-evident truth is that all men and women are brought into this world from the wombs of women in pain and travail. It is equally self-evident that the basis for the oppressive, sexual division of labor and the subjugation of women in the family under capitalism is women's reproductive function. The subjugation of women flows from dependency throughout pregnancy and while nursing – and that dependency, in turn, is actually the dependency of the human infant (which is the dependency of the human species, of human society upon women). As the anthropologist Leacock points out in her introduction to Engels' Origin of the Family, Private Property and the State:

> In some ways it is the ultimate alienation of our society that the ability to give birth has been

1

transformed into a liability. The reason is not simply that, since women bear children, they are more limited in their movements and activities. As the foregoing anthropological evidence indicates, this was not a handicap even under the limited technology of hunting-gathering life; it certainly has no relevance today. Nor did women's low status simply follow their declining importance in food production when men moved into agriculture.

Feminists have often argued (intentionally or otherwise) that biology – the ability to give birth – is the limiting factor in women's movements and activities. However, in our technological age, where it takes no more than a tiny pressure of the finger to fire an atomic rocket, program a computer or operate a typewriter, it is obvious that the biological fact of motherhood is not in and of itself the limiting factor. The limiting factors are to be found in the social relations of production and in the social relations of the family under capitalism, as Engels suggested. Engels argued that the subjugation and oppression of women can be traced to those factors which caused the communal kin group to be broken up and individual families separated out as isolated units, economically responsible for the mainten- ance of their members and for the rearing of new generations. The subjugation of the female sex was based on the transformation of their socially necessary labor into a private service for the husband which occurred through the separation of the family from the clan. It was in this context that women's domestic work came to be performed under conditions of virtual slavery. When Engels argued that the formation of the isolated patriarchal family as the economic unit of society (rather than the whole community) should be seen as the "world-historical defeat of the female sex," he in fact was identifying the institution by which the "world-historical defeat of the female sex" was accom- plished. Leacock summarizes the process:

> The significant characteristic of monogamous marriage was its transformation of the nuclear family into the basic economic unit of society, within which a woman and her children became dependent upon an individual man. Arising in conjunction with exploitative class relations, this transformation resulted in the oppression of women which has persisted to the present day.

We are not equipped with time machines, and cannot verify Engels' hypotheses concerning the origins of the "world-historical defeat of the female sex." We can, however, demonstrate that the "subjugation of the female sex was based on the transformation of their socially necessary labor into a private service for the husband" and that under capitalism the institutions of the nuclear family, monogamy (for women), the sexual definition of women's social roles, and the private appropriation of their labor power and their reproductive power are the basis of their subjugation.

If we look at the European family historically, we see that prior to the rise of industrial and monopoly capitalism, the family, as an extended kin grouping, was the economic unit of society. The family was a production unit as well as a consumer unit. With the complete triumph of commodity production, the family appeared to be reduced from a production unit to a dependent consumption unit, from an extended kin organization to the nuclear family defined by contractual marriage. This transformation of the family accompanied the transformation of labor (in the family production unit) into the commodity labor power (the ability to work sold as a commodity whose price is wages). These shifts in the function and organization of the family also created shifts in the function and role of women. As the family was increasingly isolated from any visible form of commodity production, it became, in appearance, more and more isolated from the central social and economic organization of society as a whole. The reduction of the family from the central unit of social organization to what appeared to be a peripheral "private" adjunct to the "real" social organization (commodity production) resulted in the "marginalization" of women's work and the devalued (wageless) nature of female domestic labor. It appeared that the family was marginal to capital, marginal to commodity production. Thus it appeared that women's domestic labor and, by extension, women themselves, dependent upon their husbands' wages, were of little value.

This apparent dependency justified the perpetuation of male supremacy, of the husband as the autocrat of the family, of the wife as properly dependent and servile, having the status of a bond servant within the marriage contract.

However, the seeming "marginalization" of the family and women's work in the household mystified the real function of the family under capitalism: the production and reproduction of labor power. Engels wrote in Origin of the Family, Private Property and the State:

According to the materialist conception, the determining factor in history is, in the last resort, the production and reproduction of immediate life. But this itself is of a two-fold character. On the one side, the production of the means of existence, of food, clothing and shelter, and the tools necessary for that production; on the other side, the production of human beings themselves, the propagation of the species. (1)

Marx recognized in Capital that the "determining factor in history is the production and reproduction of immediate life," and pointed out that it takes the form, under capitalism, of the production and reproduction of labor power. In short, the family is not "marginal" to commodity production; all commodity production is dependent upon the family for the one single commodity on which all of capitalist society is dependent: human labor power itself.

Marx took these factors into account in the labor theory of value. The value of the commodity labor power (as distinct from its "price" – wages) is determined by the amount of socially necessary labor time required in the overall production and reproduction of labor power. In short, the labor of the entire family as a unit, including the reproduction of new proletarians as well as the reproduction of the husband's labor power, what the husband requires to rest, recuperate and strengthen himself for the next day's labor – all of this "domestic labor" determines the real value of the wage worker's labor power. The wage, then, is not properly paid for the hours which a worker spends working for the capitalist as an individual. The real value of labor power derives from the labor of the family as a unit, and is paid in compensation for the aggregate socially necessary labor time expended by the entire family in the production and reproduction of the commodity labor power. The wages of the worker, the exchange value of labor power, are paid to the unit which produced the labor power: the family. That is the labor theory of value. It is the invisible substructure of the social relations of the family. Yet, for women, the fact that it is invisible is the pertinent fact!

Institutionalized male supremacy, rooted in the social organization of the nuclear family under late capitalism, serves to mystify the actual nature of wages and the actual determinants of the value of labor power by creating the appearance that a woman's domestic, socially necessary labor is not the production and reproduction of labor power, but a private service to the husband. This sleight of hand can be accomplished because of the peculiar mystifying nature of commodity production under capitalism in which it appears that 1) only capitalist commodity production produces surplus value, i.e., is productive labor and 2) the laborer freely contracts, as an individual, for the sale of his own, personal labor power. Therefore, since the wife's labor appears to be a private service to the husband, completely separated from commodity production, it follows that her support, her children and her labor appear to be the sole responsibility of the husband, unrelated to the value of his labor power, and thus to his wages. These two factors mean that a woman's productive labor, in the production and reproduction of the commodity labor power, is mediated through the family; and her contribution to the surplus value appropriated from the husband's labor is hidden in the individual wage system of capital. When her com- modity – labor power itself – goes to market it appears as the possession of a single individual, rather than as what it really is: the collective product of domestic labor in the family. In this way the market price of labor power can be separated from the real value of labor power. Once this occurs, a woman's labor appears to be both unwaged and valueless, when, in fact, the value of her labor ought to be included in the man's wages, that is, the price of his labor power.

As a consequence of the mystification of the family (disguising the family's true function as the unit of produc- tion for labor power itself), the social relations within the family, between husband and wife, may take on the character of the social relations of capitalism. As Engels noted long ago, the wife stands to the husband as the proletariat to the bourgeoisie. This antagonism is a consequence of the mystified nature of domestic labor, and creates the false appearance of a situation typical of other forms of unwaged labor, such as slavery:

> On the basis of the wages system even the unpaid labor seems to be paid labor. With the slave, on the contrary, even that part of his labor which is paid appears to be unpaid. Of course, in order to work the slave must live, and one part of his working day goes to replace the value of his own maintenance. But since no bargain is struck between him and his

master, and no acts of selling and buying are going
on between the two parties, all his labor seems to be
given away for nothing. (2)

Because "no acts of selling and buying are going on
between the two parties, all his (her) labor seems to be given
away for nothing"; that is, the unwaged wife is "dependent"
upon the husband for her subsistence; her wageless state in
the family reduces her to a "slave" of the husband. In fact,
she receives a "share" in the husband's wage which appears
in the mystified family unit not as her rightful share in the
collectively produced commodity, labor power, but rather as
the replacement of "the value of his (her) own maintenance."
Yet neither husband nor wife is aware of the real
(theoretical) determination of the value of labor power, and
thus face one another within the marriage contract as
"proletariat to bourgeoisie."
In the relationship within the family of (wife) proletariat
to (husband) bourgeoisie the contractual relationship takes
on a slave-like character reflective of the societal relations
of capitalism:

What the working man sells is not directly his labor,
but his laboring power, the temporary disposal of
what he makes over to the capitalist....This is so
much the case that I do not know whether by the
English laws, but certainly by some continental laws,
the maximum time is fixed for which a man is
allowed to sell his laboring power. If allowed to do
so for any indefinite period whatever, slavery would
be immediately restored. Such a sale, if it com-
prised his lifetime, for example, would make him at
once the lifelong slave of his employer. (3)

The hostility generated between husband and wife in the
family stems from the mystification which results in making
a wife the "lifelong slave of his (her) employer" because
there is no fixed, maximum time, but rather an indefinite
period, in which the wife is expected to work for the
husband. This mystification serves capital well, for it not
only ensures cheap labor (since the labor power of women as
wives does not have to be compensated at its real value), but
it also displaces a woman's hostility and frustration away
from capital and onto her husband. Both husband and wife in
the proletariat are thus cheated and tricked by capital for
the benefit and the purposes of capital. The system is all

the more vicious because it serves to make the husband an unwitting accomplice of capital in the subjugation and exploitation of women.

Let us examine the benefit to capital. Essentially, the system permits the capitalist to undervalue labor power, that is, to purchase the commodity labor power at a price (wages) far below its real value. This is accomplished only through the unrecognized nature of women's domestic labor. To show the extent of this undervaluation, let us estimate what the same labor power would bring on the open market.

A 1970 Chase Manhattan study shows that a married woman's average working week is nearly 100 hours.

Job	Hours per Week	Rate per Hour	Value per Week
Nursemaid	44.5	$2.00	$ 89.00
Housekeeper	17.5	3.25	56.88
Cook	13.1	3.25	42.58
Dishwasher	6.2	2.00	12.40
Laundress	5.9	2.50	14.75
Food Buyer	3.3	3.50	11.55
Gardener	2.3	3.00	6.90
Chauffeur	2.0	3.25	6.50
Maintenance Man	1.7	3.00	5.10
Seamstress	1.3	3.25	4.22
Dietician	1.2	4.50	5.40
Practical Nurse	0.6	3.75	2.25
	99.6		$257.53

For working-class women, the time allotments and their "value per week" would have to be even greater. The very unwaged, private and contractual relationship in the family has meant that domestic labor has remained labor intensive. The rationalization and technological development of the means of production in the domestic sphere have remained primitive since neither competition nor wage pressures operate there. Since no wages are paid, the labor time can take on an "indefinite" character. Since no commodities are exchanged between husband and wife, even that part of the wife's labor which is paid appears unpaid. All of this takes on the mask of "domestic slavery" and the husband appears as a "slave master."

The real nature of women's work in the family becomes absolutely clear when we realize that married-female labor properly falls into the service sector. Thus, if a woman works for wages as a housekeeper, waitress, laundress, seamstress, babysitter, cleaning woman, maid, companion, etc., she is counted as a part of the waged proletariat. It is only when a woman is married that such labor is defined as the "production of use values outside of capitalist commodity production." Therefore, it is not how or what is produced, it is the marriage contract that determines if female labor is waged or unwaged! It is the status wife that reduces women to unwaged and valueless labor. It is the marriage contract that gives the husband the legal right to the direct appropriation of female labor power at subsistence cost and without wages as a private service legally owed to him by his wife.

We may now also understand that much of the service sector, like the housewife, does not simply produce "use values," but, in fact, aids in the production of the basic commodity labor power insofar as the service sector contributes to the reproduction of labor power. In short, much of the service sector of the economy performs "women's work," substituting for a "wife" in the case of unmarried workers.

Women's unwaged labor in the home is the very bulwark of cheap labor costs. Is it any wonder that vast sums are spent ensuring the education and conditioning of women into acceptance of this arrangement? For the vast sums spent in education and advertising are a pittance compared to what it would cost to meet the real value of female domestic labor power.

For husbands, supporting a wife at subsistence is a very good deal, for his wages alone would not meet expenses (not to mention personalized service) of at least $250.00 per week to pay for the comfort and well-being of himself and his children. That is precisely why so many men, not realizing the mystified nature of both wages and women's labor, have remained champions of the family and "woman's place is in the home" – champions for the sake of the real, tangible, material benefits of having at hand, objectively, nothing less than a type of slave labor.

However, the benefits to capital are not yet exhausted. Because of the mystified nature of women's labor, capital is able to consistently and increasingly undervalue the price of waged labor to the point where, in the modern economy, only privileged strata of the proletariat and the middle classes are able to earn take-home wages sufficient to rear a family and support a wife at an acceptable "above the poverty line" standard of living. Most wages are so undervalued that married women are driven into the workforce in order to maintain the family. This facilitates capital's utilization of female labor in the industrial reserve army to undercut male wages while still collecting the benefits of women's unwaged domestic labor. In short, working women are super-exploited when they enter the labor force: first, through the direct appropriation of surplus value in commodity production, and then a second time through the indirect (mediated through the family) appropriation of value from domestic labor.

Conclusion

Therefore, it is fundamentally the institution of the nuclear family as it exists under capitalism and the consequent limitations of a woman's "proper" function in the production and reproduction of the proletariat (motherhood) that facilitates capital's super-exploitation of female labor in capitalist commodity production. The labor theory of value holds that wages at real value comprise the costs of the production and reproduction of labor power. Inflation, unemployment and undervalued labor power (depressed wages) exert a constant pressure to force women out of the home and into the labor force. This has always been characteristic of capitalism, as Marx pointed out long ago, but today the employment of women is steadily increasing. Furthermore, working-class women are constantly circulating through the labor force: 1) women work before marriage and during early marriage; 2) women leave the labor force when their children are in infancy and early childhood; and then 3) they return to the labor market when their children reach late childhood or are grown. This rhythm is upset anytime there are contractions and expansions of employment and wage levels. Contraction and expansion of wage levels operate to regulate the utilization of female labor as a part of the industrial reserve army. Women tend to be forced into the labor market: 1) when there is a demand for greater masses of labor power; and/or 2) when demands for cheap labor power can be met by women's undervalued wages or women's part-time work. Conversely, women are forced out of the labor market in periods of glut on the market simply because they can be reabsorbed into the nuclear family.

The circulation of women through the waged labor force, women's principal identification of themselves as wives and mothers and thus only "temporary workers" (which produces negative or very weak class consciousness), and institutionalized discrimination against women all serve to facilitate the super-exploitation of women under capitalism. This super-exploitation is expressed by: 1) the denial by capital of compensation for labor consumed in production and reproduction of labor power; 2) the systematic undervaluation of waged female labor; 3) forcing women disproportionately into the worst and most degrading jobs; and 4) forcing women into part-time or full-time work in addition to full responsibility for domestic labor (thus married working women hold down two full-time jobs, but are paid wages for only one).

Upon investigation, working-class women are clearly the most oppressed, super-exploited sector of the entire proletariat. The greatest burdens are carried by racial and national minority women. The root of women's subjugation and exploitation is not the human family as such, but the nuclear family as it is organized and exploited under advanced capitalism.

> The servant or wife should not only perform certain offices and show a servile disposition, but it is quite as imperative that they should show an acquired facility in the tactics of subservience – a trained conformity to the canons of effectual and conspicuous subservience. Even today it is this aptitude and acquired skill in the formal manifestations of the servile relation that constitutes the chief element of utility in our highly paid servants, as well as one of the chief ornaments of the well-bred housewife....It is of course sufficiently plain, to anyone who cares to see, that our bearing towards menials and other pecuniarily dependent inferiors is the bearing of the superior member in a relationship. (4)

Nor should Marxists ignore an early American socialist woman:

> To have a whole human creature consecrated to his direct personal service, to pleasing and satisfying him in every way possible – this has kept man selfish beyond the degree incidental to our stage of social growth....Pride, cruelty, and selfishness are the vices of the master; and these have been kept strong

in the bosom of the family through the false position
of women. (5)

The conflict between men and women, husbands and
wives, is not some "petty bourgeois feminist plot" to divide
the working class, but a real product of the cruel and
exploitative social relations of capitalism. In fact, no
sphere of a working-class woman's life is free from
exploitation facilitated by institutionalized male supremacy.

NOTES

1. Friedrich Engels, The Origin of the Family, Private Property
   and the State (Moscow, Progress Publishers, 1972), pp. 5-6.
2. Karl Marx, Wages, Price and Profit (Peking, Foreign Languages
   Press, 1973), p. 51.
3. Ibid., p. 44.
4. Thorstein Veblen, The Theory of the Leisured Class (New York,
   Viking Press, 1964), p. 105.
5. Charlotte Perkins Gilman, Women and Economics (New York,
   Harper and Row, 1966), p. 338.

Wages for Housework
and Strategies of
Revolutionary Fantasy

The great merit of Selma James and Mariarosa Dalla Costa's The Power of Women and the Subversion of the Community is their challenge of certain Marxist views that the "capitalist family did not produce for capitalism, was not part of social production, (so that) it followed that they repudiated women's potential social power...." and the consequence of that kind of analysis, which makes housewives socially "invisible" in proletarian struggle, and leaves the massive laboring population of women in the home virtually outside of the organizations and struggles of the proletariat.

While we owe a debt to James and Dalla Costa for raising the general level of debate on the entire question of women under capitalism, we are still constrained to engage in debate if we find the analysis to be incorrect. I do believe that the analysis is incorrect. Furthermore, I believe that it leads to strategic consequences which in

practice are self-defeating and divisive. This commentary
will focus upon the strategic consequences of the analysis.

The Mystery of Wages

Their analysis suffers from two catastrophic errors. The
first is the assertion that women's work is "unwaged" and the
second is that the family is really a "social factory." The
heart of the problem is our understanding of what the family
under capitalism is. While we do not accept that it is a
"factory," we do accept that it is a production unit. Under
capitalism the family produces a commodity, human labor
power (an individual's ability to work which is sold as a
commodity, so that the seller has no claim on the product of
his labor, and which must be produced like any other
commodity). If we follow the labor theory of value, the
value of human labor power is equivalent to the amount of
socially necessary labor time required to produce and
reproduce it. Thus the value of human labor power is based
upon all the socially necessary labor time expended by the
entire family, to feed, clothe, rest, recreate, comfort,
restore and educate those individuals taking their labor
power to market.

The value of labor power is thus determined by the labor
that it took, in the family unit, to produce and reproduce it
in the first place. However, under capitalism, the origin of
the value of labor power as determined by the collective
labor of family members is mystified, disguised, hidden by
the individualized and contractual relations under which
labor power is bought and sold. Thus, it appears that when
individual workers, male or female, contract with a capitalist employer to sell their labor power they do so as free
individuals selling the commodity of their ability to work, in
the same way that capitalists as private owners sell their
commodities (produced by the workers, but upon which the
workers have no claim). However, in reality, a wage (the
price of labor power, which is not the same as the real value
of labor power) belongs to the unit which produced the
commodity, the family (which basically means the housewife
and her domestic labor). It is because of the mystifying
capitalist relations in which labor power is bought and sold
in the labor market that the wage appears to be paid only to
an individual worker.

This mystification leads to the relationship within the
marriage contract in which the wife appears to be dependent
upon her husband's productive labor (labor power that

produces surplus value for the capitalist) and secondly, that the wage "belongs" to the husband alone, and is therefore his by right, and his to control. The wife thus appears to stand "outside" of capitalism: her work belongs to her husband (in return for her board and room), is no more than the production of use values (work which is useful but does not produce commodities), and therefore her labor is "outside" of capitalist production.

Of course, it is not true that the labor of the wife produces only use values for the husband, who then provides for her subsistence in return for these services. What is true is that the labor of the wife, and the children and every other family member who helps out in the home, are producing commodities: the one, essential, fundamental commodity under capitalism, human labor power itself! However, as long as the true function of the family is hidden by capitalist market relations in the sale of labor power, the capitalist is able to systematically undervalue the price (wage) of labor power by contracting with individual units (the worker) instead of contracting with the entire production unit (the family).

The severe undervaluation of labor power enables the capitalist to pay such wretched wages that wives are increasingly forced into the capitalist labor market, i.e., families are so undercompensated for their product, labor power, that both husband and wife must work directly for the capitalist. For the wife, this is super-exploitation: she is not compensated for her labor in producing labor power at its real value in the home, and she then is exploited a second time when she works in the labor force.

Thus, the first error in the James-Dalla Costa analysis is the presentation of the wife as being unwaged, while we have seen that her "wages" are really a part of the wages of the husband.   James and Dalla Costa reify the very mystification that serves capitalism so well! That is, they accept that the wage belongs to the husband, making the husband some kind of "boss" over the wife in the home "factory." The James-Dalla Costa analysis fails to carry out one of the principal tasks of Marxian analysis, which is to go under the appearances and mystifications produced by capitalist relations of production to the perception of the actual relations of production.   In the true relations of production of which the family is a part, the husband and wife are in fact partners in a single production process, and wages are really payment for the product of that production partnership. In short, the wife is not a dependent, but is in

<u>truth</u> a partner.

Therefore, the real task of Marxists in regard to the family is to destroy the veils of mystification which serve to 1) pit wife against husband, and 2) permit the systematic undervaluation of labor power. How can we do this? By demonstrating to working men and women, to working-class wives and families, <u>how</u> they are being cheated by the capitalists and how the capitalists have turned wives against husbands to keep wives from turning on the real <u>bosses</u> and <u>thieves</u> and <u>oppressors:</u> the capitalists. In <u>this</u> way, working-class husbands can come to understand that the price of petty tyranny over a wife is perpetual impoverishment; wives can come to understand that the husband is not a "boss" and not the real oppressor and that the impoverishment of the entire family is a product of the capitalists' ability to deny the wife's and the family's rightful claim to repayment at its real value for the labor expended in producing the commodity of labor power.

Revolutionary Fantasies

These errors in the basic James-Dalla Costa analysis lead, in turn, to profound problems in strategy and tactics as they are manifested in the "wages for housework" or "power of women" movements. First, the mystification of wages contained in the analysis (in conjunction with a <u>correct</u> appreciation of the family as the unit for the production and reproduction of labor power) produces <u>in practice</u> (in the translation of written ideas into concrete action in everyday life) an antagonistic attitude towards men in general, as if working-class men were somehow "responsible" for the psychological oppression and economic dependency of wives.

Materials with this analysis which have been translated from Italian show a marked tendency to identify <u>all</u> housewives, irrespective of their social class, as "oppressed" workers. This leads to positing "woman as a class" and the conclusion that an upper middle-class woman and a working-class woman have more in common with each other as "wageless" workers than working-class wives have with their working-class husbands. The woman-as-class (or caste) argument leads to the promotion of serious divisions within the working class; it leads working-class women into disastrous alliances with bourgeois women's organizations; above all, it attacks the development of class consciousness in working-class women, serving to strengthen the bourgeois ideology of "men as the enemy" and "women as caste," which is so destructive to the struggle for the emancipation of women.

The argument that begins "If your production is vital for capitalism, refusing to produce, refusing to work, is a fundamental lever of social power" leads to a tactic-as-strategy calling for a "general strike of housewives." This argument is hopelessly idealist. It is a "logical" deduction from an incorrect analysis that results in a completely illogical revolutionary fantasy. In the first case, a general strike of housewives (a tactic which seems to have fallen upon deaf ears since it was first proposed in ancient Greece) would not bring capitalism to a halt, although it would impose untold suffering upon the few working-class households it might be visited upon. Any number of unmarried men make it to work each morning, although infants do not manage on their own with the same ease. Furthermore, in a number of industries using migrant labor, unmarried workers are herded into barracks during the week and provided with prostitutes every Saturday night in both Europe and North America.

It is not true that the nuclear family is indispensable to capitalism. Profitable and useful, yes, but where it is not profitable and useful, it is dispensed with quickly enough. Thus, a "general strike of housewives" would turn husband against wife, for such a "strike" in fact would be against husbands and children, while it would leave capitalism untouched. In fact, the capitalists doubtless laugh themselves to sleep at night thinking of such an ideal situation: to have husbands and wives fighting each other with as much energy as capital has been able to generate between black and white workers!

Finally, the very demand "wages for housework" is, in practice, reformist and counterrevolutionary. John Kenneth Galbraith has already made a plea for a program of wages for housework. Galbraith is the real spokesman for that class of technocrats whom we may thank for the "war on poverty," the "triple revolution" and other programs for the containment of possible North American proletarian revolution. As Lenin pointed out long ago in his debates with the Economists, the easiest and cheapest concessions capital can make are those around wages and economic bribes. The objective result of the demand "wages for housework" would be a reformist campaign (energetically supported by the petty-capitalist owners and editors of Ms. magazine). The demand would probably be granted, amidst sighs of relief from the bourgeoisie, to all housewives (including those "oppressed" sisters whose husbands make $50,000 a year) in the form of petty "home allowances" to housewives. The "concession" would have to come from the state, out of the taxes of the working class: thus the working-class family would not gain an extra penny. Indeed, they would lose money, because out of their taxes would come the "family allowances" for the middle and upper middle-class women. Thus, portions of the working class's wages that might go to feed families or educate children or provide health care would be used as pin money by already significantly privileged but psychologically "oppressed" women. The question of tax-fund allocation aside, such "home allowances" or "wages for housewives" would permit capital to undervalue wages even more. Far from "liberating" housewives by providing them some of their "own spending money" the real consequence would be to force even more women onto the labor market.

What James and Dalla Costa have done on the positive side is to raise the debate about the real nature of the family and the true function of domestic labor. In that regard, the debate has also focused on the biases and sexism that crept into Marxism to distort the analysis of women and of the family. On the negative side, the "wages for housework" movement has produced objectively counterrevolutionary fantasy in the place of genuine revolutionary program.

The Subjugation of Women Under Capitalism:

The Bourgeois Morality

It is clear that the nuclear family, far from being "pre-capitalist," is an integral element in capitalist relations of production. Capital leaves not the tiniest corner of society free of its domination. A simple juridical review of marriage, divorce, custody, bastardy and welfare laws, and of the laws related to sexuality, prostitution and moral life in general, all amply demonstrate capital's direct concern with marriage, the family, children, sexuality and so-called "morals." The supervision by the state of the moral life of the proletariat is directly related to the proletariat's role in commodity production, including the production of labor power itself, without which the entire capitalist society would cease to exist.

Capital and Human Reproduction

The bourgeoisie is not interested in sexual behavior or the family as such. Capital's interest is in population, the production of human labor power in proportion to its needs. The ruling bourgeoisie is very aware that capitalism could not exist without its ultimate producer and most fundamental commodity, human labor power. Capital's need to exert population control and to supervise human reproduction, and the contradictions that this entails, are sharply revealed not only in an obsession with the rate of reproduction in the poor and developing countries, but also in the abortion, birth control, sterilization and social assistance laws in North America.

To capital, the family is the economic unit charged with the production and reproduction of labor power. Women's labor power and reproductive power – the bearing and rearing of children – have economic meaning in the necessary production of capital's essential commodity. It is clear that capital views motherhood purely in terms of commodity production, as the source of the future labor pool. Women's reproductive capacities are supervised by the state because capital needs to regulate population, to control production of the product, children. These future proletarians exist only to be exploited, to labor for the entire span of their productive lives to increase capital accumulation, and to be discarded into impoverished old age when they have been used up.

Thus the laws make clear that it is not desirable, from capital's point of view, for women to control their own bodies, i.e., for women to control the means of reproduction. It is equally clear that capital uses the nuclear family, and women's subservient position as wife-mother, as the chief means to assure the reproduction of an adequate supply of labor power for future exploitation – at the workers' expense. Where once children were an economic asset (as they are now for farm families), today children are an economic liability for the working class. Capital must, however, keep the production of new proletarians at desired levels. Motherhood-as-calling, as sole definition of women's social function, and marriage as the only "normal" condition of women, serve to assure the necessary annual crop of new proletarians. Yet capital is unwilling to pay for the production of these new workers (health, education, housing, training, etc.), displacing these costs onto the working class family. Capital does not view children as the property of parents, but as its future supply of labor power. Children are no more the "private property" of their parents than a wife's labor power and reproductive power are the private resources of her husband. All returns, directly or indirectly, to capital.

The bourgeois morality serves the purpose, from the

point of view of capital, of maintaining the nuclear family and the exploitation and subjugation of women within it. As we have outlined, the actual functions of the nuclear family are to produce and reproduce labor power, absorb female unemployment, regulate the female labor supply, discipline the male labor force and regulate population. Yet, even as the bourgeois morality serves to perpetuate the ideal of the nuclear family, capital itself is battering the family, upsetting orderly proletarian reproduction and generating multiple contradictions within the fabric of capitalist society.

While the "ideal" nuclear family may be the preferred production unit for new labor power, capital itself undermines the family as is clear from the emergence of second, third and even fourth-generation welfare families often without any marriage contracts. This situation clearly indicates that the traditional nuclear family is not absolutely essential to capitalism; indeed, the nuclear family is useful in some sectors of the labor force, while not useful or functionally absent in other sectors.

For example, from the point of view of capital, the United States now faces an over-supply – a glut on the present and future market – of racial and national minority labor power, especially of blacks. The unused and unwanted minority labor supply is dumped in urban ghettos and depressed rural areas. The very fact that capital treats millions of people as unused waste products demonstrates that capitalism has no concern whatsoever for human welfare – it cares only that its production needs are met.

Compounding the situation is the fact that depressed wages and chronic unemployment have worked to undermine the nuclear family in the urban black and Latin proletariat, since many husbands cannot economically support wives and children. The expansion and contraction of welfare payments are related to population control and the over-supply of labor power. The welfare laws themselves are indicators that somebody's labor power is required to rear new proletarians (new commodities) up to a certain age and that the state recognizes the need to pay wages to women rearing children alone, at least up to age six. However, welfare and social assistance are provided almost exclusively by taxes on the employed proletariat, creating political pressures to reduce welfare – which fits in with capital's desire to reduce national minority and poor white populations by the tried and true method of semi-starvation diet and limited health care.

The contradictions which beset the family are even more unmanageable when one realizes that "mothers" are potentially unemployed wage workers. The economically forced movement of large numbers of women from childcare to the labor force puts pressure on the job market, increases real unemployment rates, and displaces men who will not or cannot compete against severely depressed wages. The result is the continued existence in the United States of the most ferocious poverty in which the principal victims, as everywhere in the world, are the children, the aged and the women.

By understanding that capitalism concerns itself only with its own problems of supply and demand in the labor market (and not morality or humanity or any value other than the profit motive), we can also understand the source of the brutality and hypocrisy that are the essence of our moral and cultural life. It is in the context of hyprocrisy and brutality that we can come to understand the true functions and nature of the bourgeois morality in late monopoly capitalism.

Bourgeois Morality and Contractual Marriage

Bourgeois sexual morality reflects property relations insofar as it defines a woman's body, the children produced from her body and her labor power as the private property of the husband or protector. From this perspective, it is clear that bourgeois morality is fundamentally a justification of the marriage contract, which itself is no more than a legal agreement giving husbands the right to appropriate wives' productive and reproductive powers.

Under the trappings of the bourgeois morality – the frail, dependent, helpless wife, the hypocrisies of romantic love, the idyllic images of the happy housewife – is a system which justifies and rationalizes the subjugation of women. It does so by mystifying the real meaning of married women's labor, convincing a wife that her labor is valueless, a mere service to compensate her husband for her dependency upon his valuable labor power. In the same way, the bourgeois morality emphasizes monogamy, chastity, modesty and obedience. These serve to ensure a woman's subservience by convincing her that it is "God's law" or "Nature's intent" that her labor power is valueless and her children belong, by right, to her husband; that her duties are, above all, service and obedience; that her acceptance of the tutelage of her husband is necessary to her survival since she and her children are dependent upon the husband's providing.

A woman's enforced dependency and her consequent subjugation is further justified in the social definition of woman as primarily a sexual object, whose principal reason for existence is in passively giving her body for male sexual satisfaction and in the bearing of his children. Laws against adultery, for example, serve to keep access to women's sexuality the exclusive right of husbands. Fidelity and monogamy have always been strictly imposed upon women while men have been permitted to violate these norms (the ubiquitous double standard). The imposition of fidelity and monogamy has always been justified morally in terms of a husband's desire to know that he is the father of the woman's children. In fact, the question of establishing paternity is only of esoteric interest. The real function of monogamy is to ensure and stabilize an individual husband's right to appropriate his wife's labor power and reproductive power. Throughout most of human history, children were valuable pieces of property, potential and real labor power, and a husband needed a "deed" (paternity) to establish his claim to the labor power of his children. Monogamy has always functioned to seclude a woman to one man as his property in order to guard against wife-stealing and to brand her as his property – since women, as with all human beings in bondage, are not above running off, depriving the husband of both her labor power and the labor power of the children she produces.

Every mechanism of social control – moral, religious, governmental – has been used to lock women into marriage and the family. The bourgeois morality for this reason creates a psychology that asserts that a woman is not psychologically complete until she has chosen her mate, that her very human nature cannot be realized without child-bearing, that her life is empty and meaningless if she is not a wife and mother – no matter what she may have accomplished. A woman who does not marry is presented as a freak, as incomplete or humanly inadequate. None of these limitations apply to men whose realization is defined in terms of work and in terms of their life outside of the family. Indeed, the power of men to actualize themselves is manifested in the double standard, by which men are thought to require many women to establish masculinity while a woman can realize herself only through a complete submission of her own will and personality to that of a husband.

Women have always resisted, always resented, for the human spirit cannot forever be locked into a servant's worldview. This is why women are depicted in popular and bourgeois culture as either pure or sluts, where evil lurks always within the Madonna-Whore.

Bourgeois Morality and Men

Marriage, with its dependent wife and children, is the principal means by which capital secures a reliable, dependent and disciplined male labor force. The husband, upon marriage and first child, is locked into a life of work if he is to be a "good husband and father," that is, a "good provider." Once the veils of mystification are stripped away, the image is Kafka's world: women, who are never permitted to dream; men, who if they dream must put away their dreams; men and women condemned to an eternal punishment – to carry the whole parasitical mass of capital on their backs, generation upon generation. The trap is made by neither husband nor wife: the wife blames the husband for her dependency, for his resentment and his harsh treatment, for his complicity in the injustice of "woman's place"; the man resents the woman for the burden she represents, the demands she has, the complaints she makes. A wife is a bribe to the husband, but she is also his chain; a husband is security to the wife, but also her prison. Thus each is to a greater or lesser degree divided against the other. And over all of this is the dead weight of capital, whose mechanisms of competition and apparatus for the production of poisonous belief turn men against women, white against black, nation against nation.

Bourgeois Morality and Class Consciousness

The bourgeois morality promotes in women a self-identification primarily as wives and mothers (or wives and mothers-to-be) and not as workers, even when they are in the active labor force. Equally, men view women workers as a species apart, not as part of themselves as workers. Furthermore, the traditional segregation between "male" and "female" work in industry, as well as competition for jobs, is a constant source of divisiveness between men and women workers. This also perpetuates the idea that women are not "real" workers, but some strange species of interloper, who properly belong at home with their children. Even though the capacity for childbearing accounts for only a maximum of 25 years of a woman's life, the whole of a woman's life is defined by childbearing functions. Single women, childless women, girls, older women, none of whom are childbearers, nevertheless are defined by the child-bearing function. This means that large numbers of women in the labor force, objectively wage workers, are subject to discrimination which is justified in terms of the wife-mother role.

The principal definition of "respectable" women as wife-mothers has been the source of low class consciousness and the limited political development of working women because, while working, they identify more as wife and mother (or wife-to-be) than as wage worker. Consequently, women relate to husbands, not to capital; to their children, not to struggles with capital; to their sexuality and not to the vast world in which they see themselves as passive, dependent and excluded. The alienated and isolated house-wife, the strikebreaking wife-mother, the apolitical, passive and submissive female workers in manufacturing are, in part, results of women's ideological submission to bourgeois morality, reinforced by complementary male prejudices and by the realities of female super-exploitation. The develop-ment of class consciousness in women is impeded materially and ideologically by the mental and physical subjugation of marriage – whether or not a woman is, in fact, married! The wife-mother social role is the basis of the whole "feminine" definition of the social and economic functioning of women in general. Subjugation historically has produced low class consciousness and a resistance to political development. Refusal to deal with the realities of female oppression serves only to perpetuate what capital wishes: <u>not to have to fear the militance of the female half of the proletariat.</u>

Bourgeois Morality and Sexuality

The bourgeois morality, as with other anti-feminist moralities which preceded it, is essentially an expression of a master (husband)/slave (wife) class relationship. Inequality and oppression are built into its very foundation. Depen-dency and inequality produce resentment and depression in wives; having dependents and the limits they impose produces hostility and resentment – and dictatorship – in husbands. The "war between the sexes" derives directly from the programmed inequalities in heterosexual relation-ships, and, most especially, from the expectations of servility, passivity and sexual repression from women. A woman's sexuality, since it has to be guarded as a private resource, and monogamy, because it ensures the woman as a private resource, produce great fear of woman's sexuality, sexual powers and power deriving from her sexual appeal.

Bourgeois morality guards the woman as property by demanding that she repress her own sexuality or that she disguise her own sexual needs and desires in order to fulfill the object expectation placed upon her. It is this demand for sexual repression and sexual submission that has made sexuality so problematic for women. Yet, discussions of the problems of sex have always been confined to women.*

The legitimacy of a concern with the problems of sexuality to women is best shown by the fact that the act of sexual intercourse is typically an act of aggression and of dominance (and often of violation) to which a woman is forced to submit. The sex act as a violation, as an act establishing the inferiority and servility of women, has its most violently brutal expression in the act of rape. Rape is a social punishment and an affirmation of male superiority and female bestiality, buttressed by the bourgeois morality's "animal" image of woman, the Madonna-Whore, as one who secretly "enjoys" her degradation and humiliation in the act of forcible rape. This is why rapists often ask their victims if they had a climax. Rape is a particularly vicious and sadistic manifestation of the general nature of sexuality as defined by the bourgeois morality – the reality under the hypocritical expressions of "sacred motherhood" and the "lady" on her asexual pedestal.

The severe alienation produced by oppressive and repressive sexual norms and ideals finds its real expression in the horrendous rate of forcible rape and child rape. Rape is an expression of aggression and hatred vented upon a social inferior; it is an act of spiritual murder even when it is not

---

* This has been true of socialist movements, where sexuality as an area of concern has been traditionally denied or ridiculed by the men of the left. Nothing speaks more clearly to the unexamined sexism of leftist men than their continuing refusal to deal seriously with the question of sexuality. In a round of letters sent to Monthly Review in reply to an article treating Wilhelm Reich and sexuality, the male correspondents were almost hysterical in their vociferous denial of the relevance of the sexual problematic to serious Marxists. The virulent condemnation of any effort to deal with sexuality, by labeling such attempts as nothing more than manifestations of "petty bourgeois decadence" is, to women, transparent in its defense of vested male interest.

accompanied by murder in fact. Against the image of the "pure and virtuous asexual woman" is the dark counter-image of woman as victim, of a creature whose slow and bloody torturing to death is a source of sexual satisfaction and pleasure.

Heterosexuality and Homosexuality

Human beings are high-order primates. Primates are not noted for displaying a fine degree of sexual discrimination, and neither is the primate homo sapiens. Therefore, it comes as no surprise that a variety of sexual styles have existed in most societies from ancient times. Homosexuality has been extensively documented in primitive communist societies, among some slave-owning classes, among the bourgeoisie and petty bourgeoisie and among the proletariat in all advanced capitalist countries. There appears to be little or no homosexuality among serfs and peasants – probably because the economy was based on family production and exclusive homosexuals don't generally make families.* In one study of 77 primitive communist societies it was found that for 64% (49 societies) "Homosexual activities of one sort or another are considered normal and socially acceptable for certain members of the community." In 36% (28 societies) homosexual activities were rare, absent or carried on in secret. In one example, homosexuality was practiced by women only.

Well-known bourgeois sexologist Alfred Kinsey has the following comments concerning the common belief that only heterosexual activity is normal for all mammals:

Biologists and psychologists who have accepted the doctrine that the only natural function of sex is reproduction, have simply ignored the existence of sexual activity which is not reproductive. They have assumed that heterosexual responses are a part of an animal's innate, "instinctive" equipment, and that all other types of sexual activity represent "perversions" of the "normal instincts." Such interpretations are, however, mystical. They do not

---

* This is probably the reason why in some third world and underdeveloped countries homosexuality is identified as a ruling-class vice.

originate in our knowledge of the physiology of sexual responses and can be maintained only if one assumes that sexual function is in some fashion divorced from the physiologic processes which control other functions of the animal body.

The attempt to define heterosexuality as the norm of human sexual behavior is an example of metaphysical science and is not based on the material facts of the diversity of human sexual styles. Therefore the moral and social meanings attached to these styles is a doctrine of bourgeois morality which has evolved with the development of capitalism, and must be understood as an element of the superstructure serving the ends and purposes of imperialism and not as a "natural order of the universe."

Historically, it is clear that the social meaning of sexuality does not inhere in the style of sexuality (homosexuality, heterosexuality and bisexuality) but in the social meanings attached to styles. In ancient Greece male homosexuality was philosophically extolled as a love between equals, far superior to the heterosexual coupling between man and beast-woman. Female homosexuality in ancient Greece was obviously a woman's response to her bestial status – a relief from the social oppression and deprivation of a woman's life. The rise of lesbianism in the modern women's movement was a rejection of both bourgeois morality and the prevalent nature of heterosexual relationships in which strong and competent women are virtually sexually ostracized by men. Sexuality and its expressions in sexual styles are so obviously linked to the specific historical conditions in any given society at any given time that it is simply absurd to argue that one or the other style is more or less "natural."

The real analytical problem lies in understanding the origin and functions of the social meanings ascribed to any given sexual style at any given time. The problem is not psychological in nature but a question of social analysis. We must therefore understand the definitions of "natural" sexuality and acceptable sexual norms in their socioeconomic context. A doctrine of rigid heterosexuality, as it evolved to its present representation in bourgeois morality, must be understood as an element in the superstructure of capitalism, needful to the ends and purposes of capital, rather than a metaphysical exercise in determining a priori the natural sexual order in the universe. Considered within its social context, heterosexuality seen as a natural absolute (in which all other sexual styles are "deviations" or "perversions") is quite obviously related to the maintenance of the family and the male supremacy around which the family is organized. Sexual control lies at the heart of the doctrine of monogamy; but sexual control also lies at the heart of the doctrine of heterosexuality.

For both men and women, sexual regulation is in fact regulation of reproduction. Thus, the enforcement of anti-homosexual laws is primarily aimed against the working class and lower petty bourgeoisie while homosexuality is tolerated in the upper petty bourgeoisie and ruling class. The selective toleration of homosexuality has, then, a class basis which preserves the material conditions beneficial to capital.

To the primate in us, sexual style is irrevelant. But sexual style is not irrelevant to male supremacy and it is not irrelevant to controlling human reproduction. Equally, the doctrine of the "naturalness" of heterosexuality and norms of rigid heterosexuality are overridingly central to the subjugation of women: they contain some of the principal justifications for sexual and social submission within the family. Above all, the doctrine of natural heterosexuality is the ideological bulwark of male supremacy.

Homosexuality and "Proletarian Morality"

The imposition of the bourgeois morality by means of religious beliefs, social norms, social legislation and education – by all the superstructural institutions of capital – has provided the controlling ideology for the promotion and justification of the subjugation of women and has been the principal means by which capital exercises social and moral control over proletarian life and consciousness. To speak of a special "proletarian morality" arising from within the working class makes as much sense as positing that the revolutionary ideas of Marxism-Leninism spring spontaneously from the consciousnesss of the proletariat. What is usually invoked as "proletarian morality" is precisely of the same order as trade union consciousness, that is, nothing more than bourgeois ideology reflected in the proletariat and adapted to its conditions of life.

The depiction of homosexuality (or indeed any concern with sexuality) as "bourgeois decadence" is nothing more than the expression of the bourgeois morality itself. The claim that "proletarian morality" condemns homosexuality as "decadent" or "perverted" ignores the bourgeois nature of

morals in capitalist society; ignores the widespread existence of homosexual practices in all social classes, including
all strata and sectors of the proletariat; fails to make class
distinctions (lumping all homosexuals into one group defined
by sexual style alone and "declassing" the whole group by
definition); ignores the real differences between the social
meaning of male and female homosexuality; and above all,
refuses to view the nature and origins of sexual style
analytically as part of capitalist society.

The result of substituting bourgeois morality for Marxist
analysis is a purely liberal debate: 1) homosexuals should be
tolerated, i.e., be given "democratic rights"; or 2) homosexuals should be condemned as decadent and be given
therapy to overcome their "bourgeois decadent" deviation
from the sacred heterosexual absolute; or 3) homosexuals
should stay in the "closet" and not bother people.

In fact, the left's attack against homosexuality is an
attack against women, for the attack invariably takes the
form of a defense of the bourgeois morality, which is a
defense of male supremacy. The left's attack provides a .
handy weapon to silence "uppity" women demanding discussion of sexual problems and the position of women, who can
thus be accused of condoning "decadence" or of failing in
their duty to maintain "unity" with men (especially
husbands), or, horror of horrors, lapsing into "bourgeois
feminism" and questioning the holy precepts of the nuclear
family.

The most destructive consequence of the left-wing
sexism has been to drive women and homosexuals into
"sexual politics." Women's Liberation itself and, later,
lesbian vanguardism were consequences of denying women
any legitimate place, as women, in the socialist left. People
were thus forced back into a fight for their social equality
and limited to a fight against their social oppression.
Women were forced to fight the left even as they were
forced to fight the capitalist society as a whole. The
consequence of left-wing anti-feminism was in this way
profoundly reactionary, contributing to the rise of reformist
and even fascist social movements. The left was in error,
for so subjective and self-interested was the anti-feminist
attack that class analysis or a class perspective was never
addressed to the women's movement. In time, women
themselves undertook to engage in a Marxist analysis of
themselves, but only after having spent years of confusion
engendered by the self-interested sexism of petty bourgeois
male chauvinists in the left.

The predominance of "sexual politics" among homosexuals can be explained in the same way as the prevalence of "sexual politics" in the women's movement — a response to the left's definition of a "whole human creature" by but one (socially defined as negative) aspect of human existence: sex or sexuality. The distaste of heterosexual male leftists for any discussion of sexuality is, in fact, a distaste for any discussion of their objective supremacy, of their oppressor roles, of the direct benefit they personally enjoy from the subjugation of women.

Let us suggest that from the point of view of Marxism-Leninism a preference for one sexual style over another is principally irrelevant, and all the more so for the general alienated state of sexual relationships in contemporary society. Opposition to separatist politics, if principled, should be based upon class analysis and political analysis. Thus, we should oppose those groups organized around petty bourgeois class-based reformist demands; we should oppose those groups that make sexual oppression the principal contradiction, whether these are groups of women or groups of homosexuals; we should oppose all those groups holding that the first priority of proletarian revolution should be "sexual liberation" (for example, the contemporary Reichians with their various forms of sex-pol therapeutic politics, etc.).

In the end, we do not aspire to make revolution in order to free people to enjoy any sexual style they please, nor do we agitate for revolution in order to justify the practices of one group or another. We struggle to abolish capital, to liberate the masses of human beings, to build a society in which our species-being can be free to seek its greatest potentiality. It is foolish and wrong to drive dedicated people into a dead end of sexual politics by defining their humanity sexually, and then, on the basis of that definition alone, bar people as "unworthy" of revolutionary struggle. It is sexism — and like all sexism, it is madness.

Left-Wing Anti-Feminism:
A Revisionist Disorder

Proletarian Anti-Feminism: The Material Basis
for the Conflict of Interest
Between Men and Women in the Proletariat

Historically, anti-feminism in the proletariat took the form of attempts to restrict female participation in the labor force. Proletarian anti-feminism was <u>not</u> the result of stubborn sexism alone; it was principally due to the lower wages paid women and the resulting competition between men and women in the labor market. The fundamental cause of the undervalued wages of women is the overall subjugation of women in society in which: 1) women's share in poorly paid jobs is much greater than that of men (due to institutionalized discrimination) and 2) wages of married women (which are held to be no more than a contribution to their husbands' earning power) are the most severely undervalued. The undervalued wages of married women put pressure on the wages of unmarried women as well. These factors mean that women's wages come to have a depressing effect on men's wages.

Consequently, the female proletariat is caught in a massive contradiction. Women are driven to work by economic necessity, by the operation of capital itself. However, one of the ways for proletarian women to escape the tutelage inherent in the nuclear family is by being drawn into waged labor. Yet, the more women are driven into the labor force, the more their depressed wages put pressure on male wages. The resulting antagonism from male workers manifests itself in demands for the restriction of female labor which replace the earlier demands for the abolition of female labor in the production process. It is basically the same mechanism of depressed wages and the same conflict of material interests which account for the antagonism between white workers and national minority workers.

Historically, then, proletarian women have been defeated by the contradictory nature of their position, by the two-fold nature of women's emancipation under capitalism. While women could emancipate themselves by going out to work, competition at the same time imposed limits on this emancipation. The historical limits have meant that in periods of prosperity proletarian women's movements have fought for higher wages and better jobs; in periods of economic crisis women have had to fight to retain the right to work.

The super-exploitation of female labor power by capital can only be countered, in terms of reform, by union organizing and protective legislation. However, historically, the principal opposition to basic reforms (equal pay for equal work and a fair wage for a fair day's work) has come from the trade unions themselves and from the bourgeois women's movement.

While demands for the right to work, suffrage and other democratic rights have been common to both the bourgeois and proletarian women's movements, protective legislation is another story. Bourgeois women want completely free competition with men because their main enemy is patriarchalism, which must be negated before they can claim an equal share of their class privileges. Bourgeois women can afford to oppose protective legislation because, on the one hand, they are usually provided with means of support beyond their own wages or salaries; while on the other hand, the best of existing women's jobs go to the women of the bourgeoisie and petty bourgeoisie who have "care, cleanliness, taste, even art, and above all, initiative." In short, they can afford depressed wages and have a competitive advantage because they are better educated. Bourgeois and proletarian women confront each other in the labor market, and bourgeois women are one of the instruments used to undercut the wages of proletarian women. This struggle, this basic class conflict, is repeated today (just as it was fought out in Clara Zetkin's day) in the campaign for the pernicious "Equal Rights Amendment" carried on by the National Organization for Women and supported by the class collaborationist labor bureaucrats.

Where the bourgeois woman seeks only to establish juridical equality and to escape the confines of the home, the proletarian woman bears in addition all the burdens of her class exploitation and oppression. This is why, for the proletarian woman, there can be no genuine female emancipation under capitalism. It also makes clear why proletarian women have put aside their own emancipation for generations, to submerge it in class struggle. However, as we shall see, "submerging" (or liquidating) the women's struggle into class struggle is not a requirement of revolutionary struggle — it is a product of left-wing sexism and the bourgeois morality in Marxism and, above all, a consequence of revisionism.

Whose class interests (excepting those of the bourgeoisie) are served by advocating the desirability of contractual marriage and the consequent perpetuation of the subjugation of women? If we look at its material basis, we find that proletarian anti-feminism is most characteristic of those strata of the proletariat whose wages are sufficient to maintain a family at an average working-class standard of living. In such strata, where wages are adequate, a woman whose labor power is privately appropriated is a real bargain, for the same services, if waged, would be totally out of reach of the men.

Proletarian anti-feminism represents the particular material interests of highly paid, unionized male workers vis-a-vis women. The subjugation of women serves as a "natural" restriction upon the employment of female labor, and thus partially controls competition in the labor force. It keeps women unorganized and powerless in labor organizations. It secures male workers the benefits that accrue to them through their right to privately appropriate female labor power as well as the psychological "benefit" of always having a woman inferior to serve as a waitress, lover and servant, securely dependent and, at least theoretically, humbly grateful. No matter how low a man might fall, his wife is lower yet; no matter how powerless a man may truly be, his home is his castle and his subjects his wife and children.

However, wage levels and employment patterns for the lower strata of the white working class and especially of racial and national minorities show that, for these strata, men's wages are not sufficient to support a family. Wife and children are not a bargain, but a crushing economic liability. The disintegration of families, the rates of desertion, the rise of second-generation welfare families – all testify to the growing masses of men who cannot sell their labor power at a price which covers the expense of a family, much less of a non-working wife. Neither the bourgeois morality nor proletarian anti-feminism serves the interests of the lower paid strata of the proletariat, since the nuclear family does not materially benefit the husband, while depressed female wages enormously increase the suffering of families.

Furthermore, proletarian anti-feminism does not serve the overall interests of the proletariat. In its espousal of the joys of the nuclear family and the virtues of the bourgeois morality, it objectively supports the ideological foundation for the devalued wages of women by refusing to recognize the material basis for the conflict between men and women in the proletariat. The division between men and women is based upon competition for jobs, part of the mechanism for the super-exploitation of women. There will never be unity between men and women until the material basis of the competition and hostility are correctly understood and eventually abolished. No reformist program for "equal wages" or "democratic rights" has ever been or will ever be able to touch the roots of the subjugation of women; nor will women ever be mobilized to fight for "deferred" emancipation – women have learned that waiting until "after the revolution" means waiting "forever." For women, as for all other oppressed people, the fight for their own emancipation begins today or it does not begin at all. So long as a rigid, dogmatic class analysis is the basis for strategy, so long as early Marxist formulations of revolutionary strategy remain dogma (even in the face of the fact that since 1917 it has been precisely the most oppressed peoples of the world who have successfully accomplished revolution), just so long will revisionism and the liquidation of the woman "question" into male class struggle remain.

Left-Wing Sexism and Marxism

The absence of an adequate Marxian analysis of the position of women is the result of the unchallenged tenets of the bourgeois morality in Marxism itself. In the <u>Critique of the Gotha Programme</u>, Marx wrote:

> The standardization of the working day must include the <u>restriction of</u> female labor, insofar as it relates to the duration, intermissions, etc. of the working day; otherwise it could only mean the exclusion of female labor from branches of industry that are especially unhealthy for the female body or <u>objectionable morally</u> for the female sex. (Emphasis added.) (1)

About this passage Werner Thonnessen comments:

> Both the concept of "morally detrimental" in the (original) Gotha Programme and of "objectionable morally" in Marx's <u>Critique</u> show that the socialists were letting their standard of morality be prescribed by the ruling attitudes of the bourgeoisie. This is all the more amazing, as Marx had pointed out in the <u>Communist Manifesto</u> that all moral relations in the proletariat flew in the face of bourgeois morals. (2)

Female labor in general is incompatible with the bourgeois ideal of the family and most particularly incompatible with bourgeois ideals of "feminity." The attitudes were unchallenged by the socialists of Marx's day. About "unfeminine labor" Bebel wrote:

> It is truly not a lovely sight to see women, even with child, vying with men in wheeling heavily laden barrows on railway construction sites; or to observe them mixing lime and cement, or carrying heavy loads, or stones, as laborers on building sites, or to see them working at washing coal or ironstone. <u>The women there are stripped of all that is feminine and their femininity is trampled under foot, just as our men, in many different types of employment, are bereft of anything manly.</u> (3)

The loss of "femininity" in heavy or dirty labor provoked only mild indignation by contrast with the outrage and moral indignation aroused by female occupations which sinned against the bourgeois ideals of purity and chastity. Bebel again:

> Finally, younger and especially prettier women are used more and more, with the greatest damage to their whole personality, in all manner of public haunts as service personnel, singers, dancers, and so on, for the enticement of the pleasure-hungry male world. This area is governed by the most loathsome abuses and the white slave-owners here celebrate their wildest orgies. (4)

It is very clear that the socialists thoroughly shared the repressive sexual morality of the bourgeoisie. Bebel's zeal in denouncing the "immorality" of the bourgeoisie resulted in a "proletarian" ideal of purity and chastity which was the very same morality to which bourgeois patriarchalism paid homage and under which lay the subjugation of women.

The liquidationist error (liquidating the super-exploitation of women by submerging it into the class struggle) goes back to the earliest days of Marxism, to Marx himself, to the Second International; it was then carried through Lenin and reached a peak of backwardness under Stalin. In this instance, sexism and male supremacy hide themselves under "proletarian morality" and a concern for the precious "femininity" and "tender virtue" of the female sex. It was only when Marx was concerned with concrete analysis that he could glimpse over his own blinders:

> However terrible and disgusting the dissolution, under the capitalist system, of the old family ties may appear, nevertheless, modern industry, by assigning as it does an important part in the process of production, outside the domestic sphere, to women, to young persons, and to children of both sexes, creates a new economic foundation for a higher form of the family and of the relations between the sexes. It is, of course, just as absurd to hold the Teutonic-Christian form of the family to be absolute and final as it would be to apply that character to the ancient Roman, ancient Greek or Eastern forms, which, moreover, taken together form a series in historic development. Moreover, it is obvious that the fact of the collective working group being composed of individuals of both sexes

and all ages, must necessarily, under suitable conditions, become a source of humane development; although in its spontaneously developed, brutal, capitalistic form, where the laborer exists for the process of production, and not the process of production for the laborer, that fact is a pestiferous source of corruption and slavery. (5)

The objective consequences of Marxists' uncritical acceptance of the bourgeois morality concerning women and concerning sexuality have been to justify and perpetuate the subjugation of women in general and of women in the proletariat in particular and thus perpetuate the material bases for the real conflict of interest between husbands and wives, men workers and women workers. Early Marxism, as a consequence of its own sexist bias, left proletarian anti-feminism, rooted in the customary division of labor between the sexes, the traditional ideals of the family, and "woman's place" at home rearing children unchallenged. The workers' anti-feminism was based upon capital's super-exploitation of women and the resulting competition between men and women on the labor market. Marxists' anti-feminism was based upon unquestioned male supremacy. It seemed to male workers that the problem of wages and competition could most easily be solved by keeping women out of the labor market. Proletarian anti-feminism was fundamentally a result of the working man's lack of understanding that the utilization of female labor power by capital was an inevitable consequence of machine industry and the drive for cheap labor. Male socialists of the day did nothing to enlighten the working class or to challange male workers' prejudice against women. The objective consequence of proletarian anti-feminism was to play into the hands of capital by keeping men and women workers divided against each other instead of united against capital and keeping women's wages undervalued. The sexist bias in Marxism, beginning with Marx, was to perpetuate the oppression of women within the socialist movement and to strengthen the forces of revisionism within the Second International.

Proletarian Anti-Feminism and Revisionism

In the history of German Social Democracy, workers who thought in trade union terms always strictly opposed female labor. In this they were hardly challanged by orthodox male Marxists. The beginning of revisionism was in the predominance of trade unionism in the German Social Democratic Party (SPD), with its contempt for Marxist theory as "idealism" and its Lassallean concentration on reforms, to be gained through strikes and ballots, with the emphasis upon ballots. An indication of the reactionary turn in the SPD was evident in its attempts to neutralize the socialist women's movement and destroy the SPD Women's Association, because the real basis for genuine radicalism within the SPD was the women and their female Marxist leaders, Rosa Luxemburg and Clara Zetkin. Indeed, Lenin's only real allies within the Second International were Luxemburg and Zetkin!

From the earliest days of German Social Democracy the bellwether of revisionism was the position of the two tendencies – Marxism vs. Lassalleanism – on the position of women, for it was to be the women who sided with Lenin in the great debates on revisionism within the Second International. It was the Lassalleans who, from the first, transformed the super-exploitation, oppression and subjugation of women into a "question." It certainly was not a "question" to the 190,000 women who were members of trade unions, the 140,000 women who were members of the SPD and the 112,000 women who read its women's newspaper. (This momentous task of organizing was achieved largely through the untiring efforts of Clara Zetkin, against the constant interference and hostile machinations of the Party's revisionist leadership.) The subjugation of women was a "question" only to the male reactionaries in the leadership of the trade unions and the Party. We therefore conclude that it is no accident in 1977, even as in 1863, 1878, 1890, 1914 and 1920, that the subjugation of women remains, to certain men, a "question."

As early as 1866 the Lassallean position was clear: before women can be emancipated, the (male) workers must be fully emancipated. Until then, it was "sufficient for the man to work" and "woman's place" was to hold "domestic sway." For example, take the discussion document from the German Section of the First International produced in 1866:

> Bring about a situation in which every adult man can take a wife and start a family whose existence is assured through his work, and then there will be no more of those poor creatures who, in their isolation, become the victims of despair, sin against themselves and nature and put a blot on "civilization" by their prostitution and their trade in living human

flesh....The rightful work of women and mothers is
in the home and family, caring for, supervising, and
providing the first education of
children....Alongside the solemn duties of the man
and the father in public life and the family, the
woman and mother should stand for the cosiness and
poetry of domestic life, bring grace and beauty to
social relations, and be an ennobling influence in the
increase of humanity's enjoyment of life. (6)

France was not to be outdone:

The woman's place is at the domestic hearth, in the
midst of her children, watching over them and
instilling into them their first principles. A woman's
vocation is great, if she is awarded her rightful
place. (7)

The general triumph of revisionism, the transformation
of Social Democracy into a state supportive reform party,
was manifested in its treatment of women. It is worth
quoting Thonnessen at length, for nothing has changed, and
the treatment of women in the SPD will be cruelly familiar
to all of us who have matriculated through the civil rights
movement, the anti-war movement, Students for a Democratic Society and the new Communist movement:

The great theoretical decisiveness and rhetorical
sting employed by Rosa Luxemburg and Clara Zetkin
in combatting the revisionist tendency in the Party
frequently induced Party leaders who were attacked
to discriminate against women by means of
malicious witticisms (they would accuse the women
of being organizationally weak – after all, what
were 140,000 women worth) while stating, on the
other hand, that things could not be too bad as
regards the oppression of the female sex if it could
find spokesmen of such quality.
    Symptomatic of this inherently contradictory
defensive ploy on the part of men were the
comments of Ignaz Auer..."The trouble is that
there are too few women comrades in the Party. I
wish there were many more. The few who have to
do all the work are overloaded and thus prone to
become bad-tempered. So it comes about that they
sometimes make life miserable for us, even though

we are not to blame."

By the use of deliberate wit, which, as the minutes record, always evoked the sought-for "merriment" of the audience, the women were put in their place....The discrimination which was deliberately practiced against women in the Party, and of which Mrs. Kahler gave examples at the Gotha Party Conference in 1896, was in this way glossed over, while the existing antagonisms concerning the theory and tactics of the Party as a whole were obscured by accusing the women of griping and not achieving anything....Auer replied to Clara Zetkin's strong attack on the Party executive in the same tone when, amidst laughter from the audience, he said: "If that is the oppressed sex, then what on earth will happen when they are free and enjoy equal rights." The merriment which the Party executive aroused through its counter-criticism served diversionary ends, by which dissatisfaction at the ruling state of affairs in the Party was ridiculed...The fact that this criticism was made to look ridiculous also meant a break with revolutionary theory; the break with this theory, in turn, affected the leading representatives of the women's movement...(Mrs. Kahler asked) "Many comrades make such a joke of the woman question that we really have to ask ourselves: Are those really Party comrades who advocate equal rights?" Such joking proved an effective means for discriminating against women's demands. It was an expansion of the patriarchism of the men and blunted the women's criticism of the Party's reformist practice... (8)

It is not common knowledge that Rosa Luxemburg was not alone in combatting revisionism within the Second International and acting as the ally of Lenin – so also did Clara Zetkin and the whole Women's Association:

...there is no doubt that the swing of women to the left, after their leadership, resulted from the discrepancy between the Party's feminist theory and its discrimination against women in political practice. (9)

Thus women found themselves in the difficult position of

being attacked on two fronts: that of revisionism and that of proletarian anti-feminism. The men of the Party had their revenge in the end. They stripped Clara Zetkin of all power, destroyed her Women's Association and so slandered her reputation that her work is virtually unknown and her name remains a bad joke. Rosa Luxemburg had stayed clear of the Women's Association in order to be able to work as a theoretician of the Party's anti-revisionist left. During her life she was denied the benefits of Party leadership and served as the butt of "witticisms." Yet, in the end, it was Rosa they feared. And it was Rosa they murdered. The ultimate beneficiary of German revisionism, Adolph Hitler, took the revisionist position on the woman "question" to its logical conclusion and established it as the State Policy of German National Socialism, proposing the final solution to the woman question: another thousand years of subjugation, another thousand years of "the woman and mother...stand(ing) for the cosiness and poetry of domestic life, bring(ing) grace and beauty to social relations, and be(ing) an ennobling influence on the increase of humanity's enjoyment of life." (10)

The long-term result of left-wing anti-feminism has been a century of struggle in which the fundamental position of women has improved as a result of overall improvements in the standard of living of the working class, but in which women's super-exploitation and subjugation have remained exactly where they were in 1863.

Anti-Feminism in the New Communist Movement: A Revisionist Disorder

The so-called analysis of the subjugation, oppression and super-exploitation of women, tagged with the insulting and sexist misnomer the "woman question," and the resulting programs advocated by the majority of pre-party and party formations claiming to be Marxist-Leninist in North America today, can be described as versions of the German Social Democratic revisionist position. Indeed, their positions on the "woman question" have not progressed beyond August Bebel's program of 1878, were they even its equal! Most, implicitly or explicitly, advocate marriage and the traditional female role while calling for "democratic rights" (usually not different from the reformist equal rights demands of the bourgeois feminist movement). Several are so opportunist as to support bourgeois campaigns that attack protective legislation for proletarian women. When they take notice of working women's union struggles they do so opportunistically, without any consideration of the central issues affecting the general emancipation of the female proletariat. Of the known formations, most condemn homosexuality as "bourgeois decadence" by making appeals to bourgeois morality, which they are able to do only by hiding behind the bourgeois morality's manifestations in the proletariat. Such carryings-on are more clearly exposed when, in complete obliviousness to the material bases of the conflict between men and women, they suggest individual solutions through individual struggle, struggle in the bedroom, as the answer to what is a massive contradiction of capitalism in the advanced countries.

The question must be asked: whose interests are served by revisionist, anti-feminist positions in Marxist-Leninist organizations? One answer is readily obvious: the interests of the bourgeoisie and the class-collaborationist labor bureaucrats. Proletarian anti-feminism has been historically linked to trade union consciousness in the proletariat and revisionism in the party. The major pre-party and party formations in the United States seem to be following the same path trod by the Lassalleans.

It is not possible to ignore another factor with respect to the party and pre-party formations in North America: the material and social bases within the formations themselves for the perpetuation of the subjugation of women. The advantages that accrue to the men of the labor aristocracy also accrue to the men who claim they are Communists (and who are, in most cases, men of the petty bourgeoisie where anti-feminism is supremely the order of the day). The hegemony of male leadership in the formation is safeguarded by practicing and advocating monogamous contractual marriage since it assures the continued control of party "wives," and all is justified in terms of "proletarian morality." In fact, as should be clear, what is being invoked is proletarian anti-feminism and all the narrow prejudices and repressive sexuality of bourgeois morality. From the time of Marx to the present, male hegemony and male supremacy in revolutionary organizations themselves have gone practically untouched, if not unchallenged. The brutality of the treatment of Rosa Luxemburg and Clara Zetkin; the sneers, snickers, jokes, aspersions; the accusations of being ugly, nasty, domineering and unfeminine; the hypocritical forms of discrimination – all are as prevalent today as they were in German Social Democracy. The so-called "woman question" is like a searchlight cast upon these movements, revealing that they preserve bourgeois ideology and bourgeois class interests within the proletariat, however much their revisionism is hidden behind quotations from Peking Review.

Any real strategy and program for the emancipation of women must attack the bourgeois institutions of contractual marriage, private appropriation of female labor power and female reproductive power, male tutelage over women and male hegemony over women in public and organizational life. Furthermore, the masses of women not employed for wages cannot be defined into invisibility because the institution of the nuclear family is held to be sacrosanct, or because trade union reformism is seen as the only mode of struggle in pre-revolutionary periods.

None of the requirements for the emancipation of women are reformist demands because none can be met by reforms. Women do require a new and revolutionary society – but it must be a revolution and a new society in which women have an equal hand.

NOTES

1. Karl Marx, Critique of the Gotha Programme (Moscow, Progress Publishers, 1971), p. 29.
2. Werner Thonnessen, The Emancipation of Women: The Rise and Decline of the Women's Movement in German Social Democracy 1863-1933 (London, Pluto Press, 1973), p. 33.
3. Ibid., p. 34.
4. Loc. cit.
5. Karl Marx, Capital, Volume I, "A Critical Analysis of Capitalist Production" (New York, International Publishers, 1972), pp. 489-90.
6. Thonnessen, p. 20.
7. Ibid., p. 22.
8. Ibid., pp. 66-68.
9. Ibid., p. 76.
10. Discussion Document of the International Workers' Association, German Section, 1866, quoted in Thonnessen, p. 20.

Monopoly Capitalism and the Women's Movement

Against the Socialist Feminist Response to Harry Braverman's Labor and Monopoly Capital

Harry Braverman wrote, in commenting upon his own work, that "the unraveling of every complex social reality requires a starting point, and it is my strong conviction that the best starting point in every case is the analysis of the dynamic elements rather than the traditional and static aspects of a given problem." Later in the same essay, Braverman observed that "Marxism is not merely an exercise in satisfying intellectual curiosity, nor an academic pursuit, but a theory of revolution and thus a tool of combat." (1)

I

The beauty and power of Braverman's ability to use the Marxian method of dialectical materialism is wonderfully displayed in Chapter 17 of Labor and Monopoly Capital, "The Structure of the Working Class and Its Reserve Armies," and nowhere more eloquently or clearly than in his analysis of the working class:

> Labor and capital are the opposite poles of capitalist society....And yet this polarity is incorporated in a necessary identity between the two. Whatever its form, whether as money or commodities or means of production, capital is labor: it is labor that has been performed in the past, the objectified product of preceding phases of the cycle of production which becomes capital only through appropriation by the capitalist and its use in the accumulation of more capital....That portion of money capital which is set aside for the payment of labor, the portion which in each cycle is converted into living labor power, is the portion of capital which stands for and corresponds to the working population, and upon which the latter subsists.
> Before it is anything else, therefore, the working class is the animate part of capital, the part which will set in motion the process that yields to the total capital its increment of surplus value. As such, the working class is first of all raw material for exploitation....Since, in its permanent existence it is the living part of capital, its occupational structure, modes of work, and distribution through the industries of society are determined by the ongoing processes of the accumulation of capital. It is seized, released, flung into various parts of the social machinery and expelled by others, not in accord with its own will or self-activity, but in accord with the movement of capital. (2)

Braverman does us the great service of providing an adequate understanding of who and what the working class is; that understanding is critical to the development of all working-class struggles in this country. Formally, the working class is "that class which, possessing nothing but its power to labor, sells that power to capital in return for its subsistence."

The publication of Labor and Monopoly Capital marks the appearance of a genuine Marxian class analysis of the United States. The power of a Marxian analysis is demonstrated by its predictive power. No other work shows greater promise of this capacity; Braverman describes not only the present, but also those processes that lead to the probable future. In describing the probable future, Braverman meets the Marxian criterion of praxis, "theory as a tool of combat," for it is the future that dictates the practice of revolutionaries in the present. It is this analysis of processes leading to the future, and therefore strategies for the present, that we shall examine for its relevance to the issue of the social and economic emancipation of women.

II

Labor and Monopoly Capital has come under frequent attack by a number of individuals claiming a "socialist feminist" or feminist perspective. This school of criticism is exemplified by the critique by Rosalyn Baxandall, Elizabeth Ewen and Linda Gordon that appeared in the Monthly Review special issue on Braverman's book. (3) Braverman replied to Baxandall, et al, by pointing out:

> Beyond the fact that a consideration of household work would have fallen far outside the bounds of my subject (not to mention my competence), there is also this to consider; that household work, although it has been the special domain of women, is not thereby necessarily so central to the issues of women's liberation as might appear from this fact. On the contrary, it is the breakdown of the traditional household economy which has produced the present-day feminist movement. This movement in its modern form is almost entirely a product of women who have been summoned from the household by the requirements of the capital accumulation process, and subjected to experiences and stresses unknown in the previous thousands of years of household labor under a variety of social arrangements. Thus it is the analysis of this new situation that in my opinion occupies the place of first importance in the theory of modern feminism.... Thus I have the feeling that the most light will be shed on the totality of problems and issues embraced in the feminist movement, including those of household work, by an analysis that begins not with the forms of household work that have been practiced for thousands of years, but by their

weakening and by the dissociation of an increasing number of women from them in the last few decades. (4)

Since Women's Liberation (to which Baxandall, et al, claim to be indebted) has stressed psychological oppression, and particularly the psychological oppression of petty bourgeois housewives, to the exclusion of any genuine class understanding, it has become fashionable in feminist circles to center concern almost exclusively on the ideology of sexism and the organization of the family. This leads Baxandall, et al, to criticize Braverman for paying insufficient attention to the "female" experience of working women and to ignore the issue of "unwaged" labor in the home. In his reply to this critique, Braverman displays an understandable impatience with his critics' failure to grasp his analysis of the impact of monopoly capitalism upon women, the family and household labor.

Braverman's analysis of the family and household labor is found in Chapter 13, "The Universal Market." The chapter begins with a review of the history of household use value production (things and services produced for human use, but not for sale on the market) which continued throughout the early period of industrialization. Most household goods (clothing, food and household artifacts) were produced by the family unit. However, with the expansion of capital accumulation (and therefore the expansion of manufacture) the home production of use values began to be increasingly supplanted by cheap manufactured goods. It was quite literally cheaper to buy ready-made clothes than to manufacture them at home; it was cheaper to buy milk in a bottle than to keep a cow. In this way soap-making, brewing, churning, baking, preserving, spinning, weaving, tin-smithing, cheese-making, bread-making and a host of other productive home activities have been "rendered uneconomic as compared with wage labor by the cheapening of manufactured goods, and this, together with all the other pressures bearing on the working-class family, helps drive the woman out of the home and into industry."

With both husband and wife, and often children as well, drawn into wage labor, the service functions of the family also became gradually supplanted by commodity services: hospitals, old folks' homes, paid entertainment, paid sports, public schools. This constant pressure of the expansion of capital accumulation has resulted in the conversion into a commodity of every product of human labor, with the result that goods-producing labor is carried on in none but its capitalist form:

> But the industrialization of food and other elementary home provisions is only the first step in a process which eventually leads to the dependence of all social life, and indeed of all the interrelatedness of humankind, upon the marketplace....Social artifice has been destroyed in all but its marketable forms. Thus the population no longer relies upon social organization in the form of family, friends, neighbors, community, elders, children, but with few exceptions must go to market and only to market, not only for food, clothing and shelter, but also for recreation, amusement, security, for the care of the young, the old, the sick, the handicapped. In time not only the material and service needs but even the emotional patterns of life are channeled through the market. (5)

In the period of monopoly capitalism, the first step in the creation of a universal market is the conquest of all goods production by the commodity form; the second step is the conquest of services and their transformation into the commodity form; the third step is the creation of a "product cycle" which invents new goods and services and so expands the market for them. Under monopoly capitalism the market has become universal: it has destroyed all alternatives to the market. This conquest was at the expense of the traditional household economy, for the universal market of our age has meant that "the function of the family as a cooperative...way of life is brought to an end, and with this its other functions are progressively weakened." (6) This is what Braverman means when he says that it is the breakdown of the traditional household economy that is relevant for women.

How shall we now understand Braverman's assertion that the present-day feminist movement "in its modern form is almost entirely a product of women who have been summoned from the household by the requirements of the capital accumulation process"? This refers, in the first instance, to the 33 million women who presently make up 40 percent of the entire labor force, and in the second instance, to the weakening of the function of household work and the dissociation of an increasing number of women from it.

Since we began with a critique of a critique, derived from Women's Liberation, which accused Braverman of omitting a consideration of housewives, let us now discuss the housewife (whether she is working or not). The housewife is at the very nexus of the changes: the disintegration of the family and family life.

> Just as in the factory it is not the machines that are at fault but the conditions of the capitalist mode of production under which they are used, so here it is not the necessary provision of social services that is at fault, but the effects of an all-powerful market-place....As the advances of modern household and service industries lighten the family labor, they increase the futility of family life; as they remove the burdens of personal relations, they strip away its affections; as they create an intricate social life, they rob it of every vestige of community and leave in its place the cash nexus. (7)

For modern woman, the cash nexus means that she is a consumer, not a producer; it means that she is economically dependent upon the husband (unless she is working) and appears to be more of a burden than a contributor in her own right; it means that her home function is primarily child-rearing, and even that fuction is being eroded by the proliferation of commodity child-rearing services; it means that her labor in the home is principally that of an endless round of maintenance, much of it useless (does the family really care if there are six coats of super-gloss on the kitchen floor?). These are the conditions of life that create the housewife's "illness without a name," that so degrade household labor as to make it intolerable. It is the nature of human beings to attempt to realize their human potential through labor; just as rationalization degrades industrial labor, so the sheer futility of modern household labor leads to frustration and depression.

Therefore, it is the disintegration of the family and of traditional household labor – the futility and paucity of social relations – that produces the profound dislocation and rebellion of women subjected to it. Indeed, we are in a period of transition between the older form of the family and some new form arising out of the conditions of monopoly capitalism. Since the norms and values of social life change more slowly than do the material conditions of life, rebellion arises when individuals attempt to realize social values and fail. A woman believes she should be a wife and homemaker: but a wife is a non-productive dependent, and a "homemaker" is in fact an unpaid housekeeper.

Many millions of women are drawn into waged labor because home labor is uneconomic and because additional wages are needed to buy the commodity goods and services upon which the family depends. Home maintenance is the extra burden carried by working women, although increasingly husband and wife share the burdens of housework. It is the women remaining in the home who suffer the brunt of the disintegration of the traditional family; it is also these women who see their home labor as little more than "unpaid service work." The so-called "wages for housework" argument is very persuasive because housework (and often childcare) takes on the character of alienated labor, the more so as service work identical to that of the housewife is turned into waged work and commodity services. However, we must always distinguish between what is persuasive and what is accurate. The "wages for housework" argument ignores capitalist relations of production:

> According to the statistical conventions of economics, the conversion of much household labor into labor in factories, offices, hospitals, canneries, laundries, clothing shops, retail stores, restaurants, and so forth, represents a vast enlargement of the national product. The goods and services produced by unpaid labor in the home are not reckoned at all, but when the same goods and services are produced by paid labor outside the home they are counted. From a capitalist point of view, which is the only viewpoint recognized for national accounting purposes, such a reckoning makes sense. The work of the housewife, though it has the same material or service effect as that of the chambermaid, restaurant worker, cleaner, porter, or laundry worker, is outside the purview of capital; but when she takes one of these jobs outside the home she becomes a productive worker. Her labor now enriches capital and thus deserves a place in the national product. This is the logic of the universal market. (8)

Thus, the "wages for housework" argument misunderstands the relationship between husband and wife. The critical point here is that unpaid household labor does not directly contribute to capital accumulation (the definition of a "productive" worker under monopoly capitalism – see Chapter 19, "Productive and Unproductive Labor"). Household work may be a service to the husband, but to turn that into a commodity service, the housewife would have to become the employee of a capitalist, as the husband does not accumulate capital through his wife's household labor, and therefore is not an "employer" (does not appropriate surplus value or purchase his wife's labor power). If, for example, the wife were employed by a commercial housekeeping business, the husband paid the business a fee, and the business returned a portion of the fee (less the surplus value) to the wife, then it could be possible to pay "wages for housework."

If the program of the "wages for housework" movement were put into practice, it could not amount to more than a government dole to housewives (which would be extracted from working-class taxation – a disguised tax on the employed working class, male and female). This would benefit the housebound wife (much more likely to be petty bourgeois) at the expense of the working-class wife, for what capital gives with one hand it takes away with the other. If the government dole were not the source of the "wages" for housewives; then the program could demand no more than a regular allowance paid by the husband to the wife in return for her housework. How the payment of such allowances could be enforced by a state that cannot even manage to enforce the payment of child support escapes me. Furthermore, "wages for housework" is a regressive demand, one that reinforces a degraded form of household labor. Women are better advised to grasp the emerging and contradictory nature of family and motherhood under capitalism, for, at a horrendous price to be sure, monopoly capitalism is freeing women from the bonds of economic dependence and degraded household labor. Amidst the most fearful exploitation, monopoly capitalism also establishes the material basis for the social equality of women.

Although it was estimated in 1968 that household labor done by women would be equivalent to one-fourth of the U.S. gross national product (not to mention 14.2 billion dollars' worth of volunteer work, mostly in the field of social services), (9) unwaged household work is the production of use values, and as such, is "unproductive" (unproductive in that it does not directly contribute to capital accumulation). It is for this reason that the tendency from the very beginning of industrial capitalism has been to transform use values produced by household labor into commodity products and services, <u>disintegrating the family in the process</u>. The growth of the universal market really portends the increasing commercialization of the remaining areas of household labor, for the equivalent of one-fourth of the U.S. gross national product is a large kettle of potential profit! And this indeed <u>is</u> the tendency, from microwave ovens, Stouffer's gourmet frozen dinners (or McDonald's and Doggie Diners) to California Homemakers, Inc.

Thus, as the development of market relations substitutes for individual and community relations, as the social and family life of the community are weakened, new branches of production are brought into being to fill the resulting gap; and as these new services and commodities provide substitutes for human relations in the form of market relations, social and family life are further weakened. This is a process that both calls forth a very large service employment (and new service industries) to further supplant household use value production and draws ever-larger numbers of women into waged employment, while women's waged employment creates the need for even more services. The growth of the service sector is the decline of the family, and the decline of the family is both cause and result of capital's pressure upon women "who have been summoned from the household by the requirements of the capital accumulation process, and subjected to experiences and stresses unknown in the previous thousands of years of household labor...." (10)

> The ebbing of family facilities, and of family, community and neighborly feelings upon which the performance of many social functions formerly depended, leaves a void. As the family members, more of them now at work away from the home, become less and less able to care for each other in time of need, and as the ties of neighborhood, community, and friendship are reinterpreted on a narrower scale to exclude onerous responsibilities, the care of humans for each other becomes increasingly institutionalized....
>
> (The growth of such institutions calls forth a very large "service" employment.) It is characteristic of most of the jobs created in this "service sector" that, by the nature of the labor processes they incorporate, they are less susceptible to technological change than the processes of most

goods-producing industries. Thus while labor tends to stagnate or shrink in the manufacturing sector, it piles up in these services and meets a renewal of the traditional forms of pre-monopoly competition among the many firms that proliferate in fields with lower capital-entry requirements. Largely nonunion and drawing on the pool of pauperized labor at the bottom of the working-class population, these industries create new low-wage sectors of the working class, more intensely exploited and oppressed than those in the mechanized fields of production.

This is the field of employment, along with clerical work, into which women in large numbers are drawn out of the household. (11)

For socialists, the contemporary problem is to concentrate precisely upon those "experiences and stresses" that are a product of the summons to waged labor. The future of working-class* women's struggle does not lie in a rebellion against housework but in a rebellion against women's utilization in the labor force, that is, a working-class rebellion against the exploitation of waged labor.

---

* By "working class" I do not mean 1) 90% of the population; 2) everyone who works for wages or is dependent upon someone who works for wages. By working class I mean precisely "craftsmen, clerical workers, operatives, sales workers, service workers, and nonfarm laborers," Braverman's description in Chapter 17, "The Structure of the Working Class." In Chapter 18, "The 'Middle Layers' of Employment," Braverman dismisses the so-called "new working class" theory so prevalent among the self-identified socialist feminists. While it is true that members of the stratum embracing the engineering, technical and scientific cadre, the lower ranks of supervision and management, and considerable numbers of specialized and "professional" employees occupied in business and outside of capitalist industry proper, in hospitals, schools, government administration and so forth, are employed by capital for wages, they cannot be considered to be part of the working class:

All in all, therefore, those in this area of capitalist employment enjoy, in greater or lesser degree depending upon their specific place in the hierarchy, the privileges of exemption from the worst features of the proletarian situation, including, as a rule, significantly higher scales of pay. (12)

NOTES

1. Harry Braverman, "Two Comments," Monthly Review (Vol. 28, no. 3, July-August 1976), pp. 120, 122.
2. Harry Braverman, Labor and Monopoly Capital (New York, Monthly Review Press, 1974), pp. 377-78.
3. Rosalyn Baxandall, Elizabeth Ewen and Linda Gordon, "The Working Class Has Two Sexes," Monthly Review (Vol. 28, no. 3, July-August 1976).
4. Braverman, "Two Comments," p. 120.
5. Braverman, Labor and Monopoly Capital, p. 276.
6. Ibid., p. 277.
7. Ibid., p. 282.
8. Loc. cit.
9. Juanita Kreps, Sex in the Marketplace (Baltimore, Johns Hopkins Press, 1971), p. 67 and Doris Gold, "Women and Voluntarism," in Vivian Gornick and Barbara Moran, eds., Woman in Sexist Society (New York, Signet Books, 1972), p. 534.
10. Braverman, "Two Comments," p. 120.
11. Braverman, Labor and Monopoly Capital, pp. 279-82.
12. Ibid., p. 407.
13. Ibid., p. 405.

But it is not merely that the wages are higher, but rather that:

> Their pay level is significant because beyond a certain point, like the pay of the commanders of the corporation, it clearly represents not just the exchange of labor power for money – a commodity exchange – but a share in the surplus produced. (13)

The members of the "new middle class" do not sell their labor power to capital in return for subsistence; their wages, therefore, represent a portion of the surplus value produced. To be sure, segments of this "new middle class" are being proletarianized and are responding to the process with their own version of petty bourgeois radicalism – but that does not make them working class today (although a somewhat distant tomorrow is clearly on the agenda) no matter how much they insist that the college professor is no different from the office help.

The working class, then, is made up of craftsmen, clerical workers, operatives, sales workers, service workers and nonfarm laborers.

CRITIQUES OF
THE WOMEN'S MOVEMENT

The Rise and Demise of Women's Liberation

The Sisterhood Ripoff

The Rise and Demise
of Women's Liberation:
A Class Analysis

The history of the rise and demise of Women's Liberation is a primer for a study of the fatal weaknesses that infected all the New Left struggles of the 1960s. The collapse of Women's Liberation shortly followed the general collapse of the New Left in the early 1970s. Hindsight makes clear that the fatal flaw of the New Left lay in its inability to recognize the determinative role of class conflict. It was consequently unable to distinguish between class antagonisms within mass movements, a product of the failure to comprehend that revolutionary movements arise and flourish only within revolutionary classes.

Many of the errors of the New Left are perpetuated today, whether it be in the so-called socialist feminist

Portions of this article were published under the title "Women's Liberation: Opening Chapter Two," in Canadian Dimension, Vol. X, No. 8, 1975.

movement or in the so-called anti-imperialist movement. Each such tendency, in its own way, has failed to learn from the recent past. Yet, as women, we must not fall prey to the dictum "history repeats itself," for the massive institutionalized exploitation and oppression of women continues, virtually untouched by all the fulminations of the 1960s, just as American imperialism flourishes with unhampered brutality. Nevertheless, any critique of the New Left must recognize that it was, in itself, a powerfully progressive force in all of its manifestations.

Consequently, we cannot fail to recognize that the Women's Liberation movement resurrected the "woman question" and rebuilt on a world scale a consciousness of the exploitation and oppression of women. For nearly forty years women had been without a voice to articulate the injustice and brutality of women's place. For nearly forty years women had been without an instrumentality to fight against their exploitation and oppression. From the mid-1960s to the early 1970s, Women's Liberation became that new instrumentality. From the United States and Canada to Europe, to national liberation struggles in Africa and Asia, to revolutionary China itself, the reverberations of the movement set in motion a new awareness and new movements for the emancipation of women. Whatever the faults and weaknesses of Women's Liberation in the United States and Canada, it was a historical event of worldwide importance.

Nevertheless, what happened to the Women's Liberation movement in the early 1970s is precisely what happened to each mass movement of the last decade: internal differentiation along class and political lines. In the case of the women's movement, the remnants of Women's Liberation have come to be dominated by a middle class leadership, reducing a vigorous and radical social movement to a politically and ideologically co-opted reformist lobby in the halls of Congress. The problem before us is to understand the course of the class conflict that resulted in the final co-optation and decline of the autonomous women's movement.

Consciousness Raising: The Beginning

The autonomous women's movement was a necessity of the time, a product of the political realities of the 1960s, a transitional movement which was a direct product of the male supremacist structure of the New Left and the legitimacy it permitted for the expression of male dominance in everyday life. The New Left was an instrument for the suppression, oppression and exploitation of women. The formation of the autonomous movement was the only reply possible. Women set about organizing women in order to avoid the wrecking tactics of the men and to openly fight against the exploitation and oppression of women. Women would never have been able to do so within the male-dominated New Left. Women clearly recognized that the politics and practice around the "woman question" on the part of student and other left groupings were deformed by their own practice of male supremacy. Women were forced to conclude, on the basis of experience, that only by building a base among women would it be possible to put a correct priority on the question of the emancipation of women, to confront the entire left and force them to a recognition of the centrality of women's emancipation in all revolutionary struggles.

The origin and importance of the small consciousness-raising group is to be found in the basic organizing tool of the autonomous movement: organize around your own oppression. There were many foundations for such a position. First, the major task faced by early organizers was to get women to admit that they in fact were oppressed. The socialization of women includes a vast superstructure of rationalizations for women's secondary status; the super-structure of belief is reinforced through inducing guilt and fear (of not being a "true" woman, etc.) as a response to rebellion against women's traditional role; consequently, women are raised to be very conservative, to cling to the verities of the hearth, to a limited and unquestioning acceptance of things as they are. However, organizers very quickly learned that under the crust of surface submission there had built up in countless women an enormous frustra-tion, anger, bitterness – what Betty Friedan called "an illness without a name." Women's Liberation gave the illness a name, an explanation and a cure. The cure was the small group and the method was what the Chinese Communists call "speaking bitterness." The bitterness, once spoken, was almost overwhelming in its sheer emotional impact.

For many new recruits, consciousness raising was the end-all and be-all of the early movement, a mystical method to self-realization and personal liberation. But for others, especially for left-wing radical women, the original aim of the small group was supposed to have been the path to sisterhood – that unity expressed in empathic identification with the suffering of all women – which would lead from the recognition of one's own oppression to identification with the sisterhood of all women, from sisterhood to radical politics, from radical politics to revolution. Early organizers had correctly understood that women could be organized on a mass scale in terms of their own subjective oppression and by appealing to the common oppression of all women (irrespective of class). Aiming at radicalizing the constituency of Women's Liberation, early radical organizers talked a great deal about the common source of oppression (hoping to foster the empathic identification that would provide the bridge to cross-class unity). They talked much less about the fact that the common oppression of women has different results in different social classes. The result of the class position, or class identification, of almost all recruits to Women's Liberation was to retranslate "organize around your own oppression" to "organize around your own interests." The step from self-understanding to altruistic identification and cross-class unity never occurred because the real basis for radicalization, common economic exploitation, was absent.

"Organize around your own oppression" was indeed a Pandora's Box of troubles. Middle class women used this maxim to justify the pursuit of their own class interests: "We are oppressed too," "We must take care of our own problems first." Middle class women also justified ignoring the mass of working class women by asserting that "ending our oppression will end theirs," i.e., the fight against discrimination would equalize the status of all women.

The transformation of the small group from its original political consciousness-raising function into a mechanism for social control and group therapy was a result of the predominantly middle class character of Women's Liberation. The fact that there were so few women in Women's Liberation who were directly experiencing material deprivation, threats of genocide or enforced pauperization – that is, so few who were driven by conditions of objective exploitation and deep social oppression – made it almost inevitable that the search for cultural and life-style changes were substituted for revolutionary politics.

What radicals had not taken into account was the fact that middle class and wealthy women do not want to identify with their class inferiors; do not care, by and large, what happens to women who have problems different from their own; greatly dislike being reminded that they are richer, better educated, healthier and have more life chances than most people.

Therefore, behind the outward unity of the Women's Liberation movement of the 1960s, centered as it was around a public ideology based upon feminism, sisterhood and the demand for equal rights, there raged an internal fight between the so-called feminists and politicos. This fight was disguised in many ways, most effectively by personalizing it or by casting it as a battle against "male-identified" or "elitist" women, in which the pejorative "politico" implied both sins summed up by the phrase "anti-woman." All of these pseudo-psychological arguments were manipulative verbiage which mystified the fact that class politics vs. reform politics, and therefore class conflict for hegemony over the leadership of the movement, were the real stakes of the combat. Certainly, participants at the time often were not consciously aware of the true nature of their struggle, but from the vantage point of hindsight, the true meaning of these struggles is manifestly clear. While in the beginning, roughly from 1967 to 1969, the left was in a relatively powerful position, by 1973 a coalition of the center and right had gained control of the women's movement.

The Rise of Class Conflict

The early and primitive ideology of Women's Liberation stressed psychological oppression and social and occupational discrimination. The politics of psychological oppression swiftly transmuted into the bourgeois feminist ideology of "men as the enemy," for psychological world-views pit individual against individual and mystify the social basis of exploitation. Nevertheless, the politics of psychological oppression and of invoking the injustice of discrimination were aimed at altering the consciousness of women newly recruited to the movement in order to transform personal discontent into political militancy. Women, being in most cases without a political vocabulary, could most easily respond to the articulation of emotion. (This, of course, explains the impassioned, personal nature of the early polemical literature. It was indeed "speaking bitterness.") Furthermore, women of almost any political persuasion or lack of one can easily accept the straight-forward demand for social equality. Explaining the necessity for the abolition of social classes, the complexities of capitalism and its necessary evolution into imperialism, etc., a much more formidable task, often elicited more hostility than sympathy. On the other hand, the stress on discrimination and psychological theorizing aimed directly at the liberal core of North American politics. In turn, sex discrimination affects all women, irrespective of race, language or class (but the fact that it does not affect all women in the same way or to the same degree was often absent from discussion).

The primacy of ideologies of oppression and discrimination (and the absence of class analysis exposing exploitation) and the ethic of sisterhood, facilitated the recruitment of large numbers of women from certain strata of the middle class, especially students, professionals, upper-middle class housewives and women from all sections of the academic world.

Given the predominantly apolitical disposition of women in general coupled with their initial fearfulness and lack of political experience, the task of revolutionary political education was an uphill battle from the beginning. The articulation of a class analysis in both Canada and the U.S., too often in a style inherited from the competitive and intellectually arrogant student left, frightened women away or left them totally confused and unable to understand what the fuss was all about. In a purely agitational sense, the feminists' anti-male line had the beauty of simplicity and matched the everyday experience of women; the left-wing radicals had the disadvantage of a complex argument that required hard work and study, an "elitist" sin. However, the anti-male line had its difficulties too, rooted in a fundamental contradiction which faces all women. It was impossible to tell women not to resent men, when it was plain in everyday life that the agents of a woman's oppression at home and on the job were men. On the other hand, women were unwilling and unable to actualize anger against sexism into a hatred of men.

Because of this contradiction there existed a predisposition to take a rhetorical anti-male stand (throwing men out of meetings to keep them from being obstructionist, expressing anger and contempt towards men to display defiance and thus give moral support and courage to new women, etc.), overlaying a profound ambiguity regarding what was, or ought to be, the relationship between men and women.

The result was a situation which might be termed dual leadership, made up of the early left activist organizers, the politicos, and the newer level of middle class women, the feminists, the latter seeking, by virtue of their class position, wealth and education, to bring the goals, ideology and style of the movement into line with their politics and class interests. The ethic of sisterhood publicly smoothed over these two opposing conceptions of the enemy, i.e., who and what is going to be abolished to accomplish the liberation of women. Thus, the public ideology of Women's Liberation built unity around certain basic feminist tenets acceptable to the mixed class composition of the mass movement: 1) first priority must be placed on the organization and liberation of women (glossing over differing and contradictory positions on the definition and means to attain liberation); 2) action programs ought to put first priority upon woman-centered issues; 3) socialist revolution would not in itself guarantee the liberation of women.

The class conflict seething under the nominal agreement on the basic tenets of feminism was ideologically expressed in two contradictory lines of analysis corresponding to the dual leadership situation. The feminist line stemmed from the assertion that "men are the principal enemy" and that the primary contradiction is between men and women. The politico line stemmed from the assertion that the male supremacist ruling class is the principal enemy and that the primary contradiction exists between the exploited and exploiting classes, in which women bear the double burden of economic exploitation and social oppression. The leftist line stressed that the object of combat against male-supremacist practices was the unification of the men and women of the exploited classes against a common class enemy in order to transcend the division and conflict sexism created between them. Women's Liberation was called upon to combat sexism by combatting the dependency and subjugation of women that created and perpetuated the exploitation and oppression of women. The position on men was explicit: men in the exploited classes, bribed through their privileged position over women, acted so as to divide the class struggle. The source of divisiveness was not men per se but the practice of male supremacy.

One can immediately see that the leftist analysis, pointing to class and property relations as the source of the oppression of women, was much more difficult to propagandize than the feminist anti-male line. In everyday life what all women confront is the bullying exploitation of men. From the job to the bedroom, men are the enemy, but men are not the same <u>kind</u> of enemy to all women.

The Material Basis of Bourgeois Feminism

For the middle class woman, particularly if she has a career or is planning to have a career, the primary problem is to get men out of the way (i.e. to free women from male dominance maintained by institutionalized discrimination), in order to enjoy, along with the men, the full privileges of middle class status. The system of sexual inequality and institutionalized discrimination, not class exploitation, is the primary source of middle class female protest. Given this fact, it is men, and not the very organization of the social system itself, who stand in the way. Consequently, it is reform of the existing system which is required, and not the abolition of existing property relations, not proletarian revolution – which would sweep away the privileges of the middle class woman.

The fact that the fight against discrimination is essentially a liberal reform program was further mystified by the assertion that the equalization of the status of women would bring about a "revolution" because it would alter the structure of the family and transform human relationships (which were held to be perverted through the existence of male authoritarianism). The left line held that equalization of the status of women is not, nor could it be, the cause of the decomposition of the nuclear family. The organization of the family is a result of the existing economic structure; just as the origin of the contemporary nuclear family is to be found in the rise of capitalism, so it is perpetuated in the interests of monopoly capitalism. Furthermore, equalization of the status of women would be no more likely to introduce an era of beautiful human relationships than did the introduction of Christianity bring obedience to the Golden Rule or the Ten Commandments. The claim that status equalization would bring about a "revolution" is of the same order as the claim made by the Suffragists that giving women the vote would usher in an era of world peace. Abolishing discrimination would not lead to a "revolution" in the status of women because it would leave the class structure absolutely untouched. Gloria Steinem might build a corporation, a woman might become a general or a corporation vice-president, but the factory girl would remain the factory girl.

The tactical <u>and</u> ideological error of the left in this struggle was to try to win the <u>entire</u> mass movement to their position. The failure to recognize class struggles led to the defeat of the leftist position not only because of the predominant middle class background of the movement, but also because the left had not only to fight the petty bourgeois reformers, but also the anticommunist, cold war ideologies with which almost all North Americans have been so thoroughly infected. Without disciplined organization and a working class base, a left position will always lose in a mass movement, or be reduced to self-defeating opportunism.

Sisterhood: Root of Bourgeois Feminism

The politics of oppression and the politics of discrimination were amalgamated and popularized in the ethic of sisterhood. Sisterhood invoked the common oppression of all women, the common discrimination suffered by all. Sisterhood was the bond, the strength of the women's movement. It was the call to unity and the basis of solidarity against all attacks from the male-dominated left and right, based on the idea that common oppression creates common understanding and common interests upon which all women can unite (transcending class, language and race lines) to bring about a vast movement for social justice – after first abolishing the special privileges enjoyed by all men, naturally.

The ideology of sisterhood came to emphatically deny the importance, even the existence, of class conflict in the women's movement. To raise class issues, to suggest the existence of class conflict, to engage in any form of class struggle was defined as divisive of women, as a plot by men to destroy women (after all, were not Marx and Lenin men?) as weakening the women's struggle, and the perpetrator was proven beyond the shadow of a doubt, to be a traitor to women, male-identified, an agent of the enemy in the sisterhood. Sisterhood was a moral imperative: disagreements were to be minimized, no woman was to be excluded from the movement, all sisters were to love all other sisters, all sisters were to support all other sisters, no sister was to publicly criticize other sisters.

Sisterhood, and the outward unity it provided, also disguised and mystified the internal class contradictions of the women's movement. Specifically, sisterhood temporarily disguised the fact that all women do not have the same interests, needs, desires: working class women and middle class women, student women and professional women, minority women and white women have more conflicting interests than could ever be overcome by their common experience based on sex discrimination. The illusions of sisterhood were possible because Women's Liberation had become in its ideology and politics predominantly a middle class movement. The voices of poor and working class women, of racial and national minority women or even of housewives with children were only infrequently heard. Even when these women were recognized, they were dismissed with a token gesture or an empty promise. When the isolation of the left was complete, almost all internal opposition to bourgeois feminism disappeared.

The collapse of sisterhood was principally a result of the disguised class and political conflict which became acute throughout 1970-71. Under the guise of rejecting "elitism" left-wing women were attacked mercilessly for being "domineering," "oppressive," "elitist," "male-identified," etc. In fact, the early radical leadership was in this way either discredited or driven out of the movement, to be replaced by "nonoppressive," "apolitical," manipulative feminist or "radical feminist" leadership. This was the period of the "trashing." At this time a clearly defined right-wing also emerged, the reactionary "radical feminists" who were, by and large, virulently anti-leftist and anticommunist.

In the end, political debate became almost completely nonexistent in the small group, which was essentially reduced to being a source of social and psychological support. Rivalries, disputes and feuds often grew up between small groups in the same city (each doubtless accusing the other of being "elitist"), frequently having the effect (along with the major programmatic and ideological divisions between feminists and politicos) of making even the minimal workings of a women's center impossible.

Reactionary Feminism

The bourgeois feminist line, "men are the enemy," branches into two ideologies, liberal feminism and reactionary (or "radical") feminism. The first, liberal feminism, does not openly admit that its ideology is a variant on "men are the enemy" but disguises that assumption behind a liberal facade that men are "misguided" and through education and persuasion (legal if need be) can be brought around to accepting the equalization of the status of women. Since the questions of the origins of injustice and the roots of social power are never very strong in any liberal ideology, there is little besides legislative reforms and education to fall back on.

Reactionary feminism, on the other hand, openly asserted as its fundamental tenet that all men are the enemies of all women and, in its most extreme forms, called for the subjugation of all men to some form of matriarchy (and sometimes for the extermination of all men). It offered a utopia composed of police states and extermination camps, even though reactionary feminists very rarely followed through to the logical outcome of their position.

Reactionary feminism was not an ideology of revolution (the likelihood of victory seeming remote even to its advocates) but an ideology of vengeance. It was also a profound statement of despair that saw the cruelty and ugliness of present relationships between men and women as immutable, inescapable. Reactionary feminism may have been politically confused, and it was certainly politically destructive, but it powerfully expressed the experience and feeling of a whole segment of the female population.

The root of reactionary feminism was in the sexual exploitation of women. Its strength lay in the fact that it did express and appeal to psychological oppression, for this oppression is far worse than the conditions of economic exploitation experienced by petty bourgeois women. In the last analysis reactionary feminism was a product of male supremacy, and its corollary, sexual exploitation. Male supremacy, itself reactionary, breeds reaction.

With the virtual expulsion of the left leadership the "radical feminists" assumed leadership over the portion of the movement not yet co-opted into the reformist wing. The excesses of the right: man-hating, reactionary separatism, lesbian vanguardism, virulent anticommunism, opposition to all peoples' revolutionary struggles (including Vietnam), served to discredit Women's Liberation and to make public the split in the movement between the reformists and the radical feminists. Of the expulsion of the left, no mention was made, keeping up the masquerade as an "anti-elitist campaign." The triumph of the right resulted in the disintegration of the Women's Liberation movement. In the shambles to which the movement had reduced itself, left and right opportunists were swift to seize the opportunity to take control. The leftists watched the predictable occur with despair while the reactionary, so-called "radical" feminists, with their shriek of "elitism" still issuing from their mouths, found the movement they had sought to control snatched out of their hands.

The Failure of Program

Women's Liberation never produced a coherent program. Programmatic development requires theoretical development, and Women's Liberation was incapable, on the basis of its class contradictions alone, of generating a coherent political analysis. What program and agitation existed clearly reflected the class nature of the movement. The wide variety of national and local single-issue programs undertaken by isolated women's groups reflected the overriding problems of younger, middle class women: the need for legal abortion (rather than a demand for universal health and nutritional care, including abortion and birth control services, which working class and poor women desperately need); demands for cooperative, "parent controlled" day-care centers (rather than universal day-care with compensatory educational programs which the majority of working class parents and children need); the creation of women's centers to provide young women with a "place of their own" in which to socialize, to work for abortion on demand or to secure illegal abortions (rather than creating "organizational" centers capable of organizing with working class women for struggles on the job or in the community).

The cold truth of the matter is that the women's centers often differed very little from the standby of the suburban housewife – community work, complete with good deeds, exciting activities, lively gossip and truly thrilling exercises in intrigue and character assassination. Within these centers working class women often wandered about in a state of frustration and confusion. They knew something was very wrong, but they did not know what.

Given the almost exclusive attention to sexual exploitation and the consequent psychological oppression, the focus was not upon male supremacy as part of class exploitation, but upon its result, the practice of male chauvinism; not upon the need for revolutionary social and economic changes, but upon individualized struggles between men and women around the oppressive attitudes and objective sexual and social privileges of men. Furthermore, emphasis upon male chauvinism had the effect of privatizing the contradiction between men and women, transmuting the conflict into problems of personal relationships, rather than politicizing the conflict as part of the overall capitalist system of economic and class exploitation.

The internal failures of the movement may be summed up in a brief series of criticisms. Mass movements contain within them class contradictions; women were far too slow to recognize class struggle for what it was within the movement. Furthermore, lack of a correct theoretical analysis led to the left's inability to generate correct programs to guide internal class struggle. The movement was thus reduced to single-issue mass campaigns which had to coalesce around the lowest common denominator, reform. Leadership thus passed to liberal reformers or left opportunists who opposed straightforward class conflict or open recognition of the inevitability of such conflict. The movement isolated itself, for these and other reasons, from the concrete struggles of working class women, in the home and in the factory, who make up the majority of oppressed and exploited women. The final and perhaps the most important lesson to be learned is that a movement without coherent politics, organization and discipline cannot be a fighting organization.

In short, Women's Liberation, for all its rhetoric and all its pretensions, for all its brave start, has outwardly become what it really was (indeed, what it had to be): an anti-working class, anticommunist, petty bourgeois reform movement.

Socialist Feminism

The last gasp of Women's Liberation continues today as a loose collection of small local organizations committed in varying degrees to autonomous socialist feminist organizing. The constituency is almost exclusively from the white petty bourgeoisie as indicated by attendance at the National Conference on Socialist Feminism (held in 1975). Reports of the 1975 conference suggest that the socialist feminist constituency is very mixed in political orientation. There is without doubt a significant proportion of women who are biding their time with socialist feminism in reaction to the regressive positions of most new Marxist-Leninist formations (whose morality is Victorian and whose understanding of the so-called "woman question" is hardly equal to Bebel's statement written in 1879). There is reason to believe, however, that its stable constituency is made up of white radical feminists who are conscious social democrats and who represent one continuation of the radical petty bourgeois politics of the early days of Women's Liberation. Whatever the precise class composition of socialist feminism might be, its leading tendency is clearly a cross between radical feminism and social democracy. This peculiar amalgamation underlies the first three "principles of unity" drawn up by the conference organizers:

1. We recognize the need for and support the existence of the autonomous women's movement throughout the revolutionary process.
2. We agree that all oppression, whether based

on race, class, sex, or lesbianism, is interrelated and the fights for liberation from oppression must be simultaneous and cooperative.

3. We agree that Socialist Feminism is a strategy for revolution. (1)

It is not surprising that these "principles of unity" produced very little unity and a great deal of confusion and contention, also very reminiscent of the confused and contradictory organizing conferences of Women's Liberation. Nevertheless, the "principles of unity" exhibit very clearly the petty bourgeois class character of Women's Liberation perpetuated under the guise of socialist feminism. For example, in principle no. 2 we note that "all oppression, whether based on race, class, sex or lesbianism, is inter-related" without any indication of how they are interrelated. Throughout, oppression is used, but not exploitation. Oppression is a psychological term, while exploitation is an economic term that refers to class relations. Class is used as a category in itself, as are race, sex and lesbianism. There is no recognition that race and sex discrimination are products of class exploitation. We must assume that tacking on "lesbianism" is a result of an opportunist attempt to appeal to radical lesbians, for surely homosexuality is subsumed under sexual discrimination.

Hostility toward recognizing the determinative role of class, also inherited from Women's Liberation, is demonstrated in a report of the conference written by a member of the Berkeley-Oakland Women's Union:

> There was much said in panels and in workshops on the question of race, class, lesbianism, etc., but there was no agreed-upon framework in which to place these discussions. Nor was there any apparent reason to attempt to resolve differences, as we were making no commitment to work or struggle together beyond the conference....Members of the Marxist-Leninist caucus often stated that class was the primary contradiction. They also often remarked that the women's movement was a "middle class" movement. Many of the working women at the conference expressed a personal disgust at this sloppiness of terminology, as well as the way it discounted their own position in the work force....(2)

The "disgust" was displayed by those women who were

sympathetic to the position put forward by Barbara Ehrenreich:

> Let's start by being very honest about class. About ninety per cent of the American people are "working class": in the sense that they sell their labor for wages, or are dependent on others who do....Now what does that tell us?....It tells us, for political purposes, a class is not defined strictly by gross economic relationships. For political purposes, a class is defined by its consciousness of itself as a class that exists in opposition to another class or classes. (3)

The Ehrenreich position resolves the problem of "sloppy terminology" by liquidating the middle class (or new petty bourgeoisie) into a vast, undifferentiated mass (90% of the population) defined by class consciousness-for-itself. Since no such class or class consciousness presently exists in the United States, class is effectively made non-existent. It therefore follows that women can be united around their common "oppression" and become a "class defined by its consciousness of itself as a class that exists in opposition to another class or classes," and we are right back to the unity of sisterhood propounded by Women's Liberation. Is it any wonder that "the conference was also plagued with the homogeneity contradiction (sic), most of the women there being white and under thirty-five years old...."? (4) Dismissing the determinative role of social class as a "gross economic relationship" and substituting a psychological definition without a material basis perpetuates the Women's Liberation tactic of "organizing around your own oppression," exemplified by the retention of the slogan, "the personal is political." The rejection of Marxism as an "agreed-upon framework" thereby continues to justify the hegemony of white middle class (petty bourgeois) women in Women's Liberation-by-another-name: socialist feminism.

The real unity of the socialist feminist tendency is stated in the first principle asserting the necessity of an autonomous women's movement. In clinging to this belief, socialist feminism would condemn women to continued isolation and segregation. The formation of the autonomous movement in the mid-1960s reflected the constraints that pervasive and entrenched left-wing male sexism put upon any attempt to organize women as a significant part of the New Left. In organizing the autonomous movement, women had demonstrated their ability to organize a vigorous mass movement.

Yet, the male-dominated left's actual response was to isolate and ghettoize the women's movement even within the petty bourgeois left. Women's Liberation fell into the trap by characterizing political struggles as "male-dominated," or Marxism as "penis politics," reducing Women's Liberation to dead-end reformist programs around "women's issues": abortion, day-care, women's studies programs, women's health clinics and so forth. The reduction of the autonomous movement to a trivialized, isolated and limited series of local reformist struggles was the legacy of retaining a separate women's movement.

Once the "woman question" had been put on the New Left agenda, conditions were created that potentially could have enabled women to carry the fight against sexism directly into the left. By and large, this did not happen. The autonomous movement, by isolating women, did not allow a serious political campaign against sexism to be carried out between men and women as an organizational struggle. The continued political segregation of women limited opposing sexism to opposing sexism in one's lover or husband. Consequently, the autonomous movement failed in its mission of defeating left-wing sexism, as the regressive lines of much of the new communist movement make quite clear. The prolonged existence of the autonomous move-ment, with its penchant for psychological theorizing, made it difficult to see that the defeat of sexism and racism in the left was an organizational, not attitudinal, problem. The solution to the prevalence of both sexism and racism must be found in the process of party formation itself. The very structure of a revolutionary party must provide an organiza-tional basis upon which equality between comrades can be developed and enforced.

The rejection of Marxism, the rejection of the deter-minative role of the relations of production, also serves to mystify precisely what sexism is – a class relationship between the sexes, just as racism is a class relation between races. This was the insight provided by Engels so long ago, when he wrote that the relationship between man and wife was as the bourgeoisie to the proletariat. It is not that men and women, black people and white people, each make up a class (although at one time that was asserted in Women's Liberation) but rather that the social relations existing between them irrespective of actual class membership have the character of class relations, being, as they are, the product of class relations. Thus, sexism and racism have a class identity: each demands relations of inequality, subordination, and the assumed inferiority of one group of humanity to another.

The refusal to recognize the determinative role of class relations in Women's Liberation and in its offspring, socialist feminism, must result in reducing talk of "revolutionary process" and "socialist feminism is a strategy for revolution" to radical cant. These phrases can have no content, no real referent, without a unified theoretical understanding of the origins of exploitation and the material roots of psychological oppression. Socialist feminism is, in the final analysis, nothing more than a continuation of Women's Liberation past its time.

New Directions

The entire period of the 1960s in North America was crippled by the cold war repression of the 1940s and 1950s which had left two generations almost completely bereft of any knowledge, theoretical or historical, of North American class struggle and North American socialism. Over twenty years of anti-Marxist, anti-Soviet propaganda (which began in the elementary school and continued through graduate education) guaranteed that the majority of North American youth was anticommunist, antisocialist, anti-Marxist. U.S. imperialism and its Canadian branch plant protected the masses of the people from severe material deprivation and served to validate the ideologies of "America, the apex of democratic, free enterprise" on both sides of the border. Indeed, it was one of the contradictions of imperialism, the brutal exploitation of black and native people throughout the continent and of Quebecois in Canada, which began the revival of a moribund left and signaled the sharpening of the contradictions and class struggle which marks the 1970s.

Isolation from revolutionary theory and practice left the movement, specifically the New Left, the peace movement and Women's Liberation, without the theoretical tools (and most particularly without any understanding of dialectical analysis) so necessary to guide practice in the long run. As a result, practice was typically pragmatic and sporadic, marked by few victories and many defeats, exhausting and disillusioning people. Isolation from revolutionary classes, combined with theoretical and historical ignorance, meant that people often did not have any adequate analysis. As a result, people were tactically, not strategically oriented. Furthermore, they were populist and reformist by default, through ignorance and programmed anticommunism. Great numbers of militants responded with confusion and despair as effort after effort collapsed or was defeated outright or, even more frustrating, was co-opted into irrelevant reform. Without any knowledge or sense of the dialectics of history, without a correct understanding of capitalism and imperialism, with no way to evaluate or understand the course of class struggle, the radicalism of the 1960s found itself bankrupted in a few short years. Thus, we can clearly see that Women's Liberation was not unique, but that the fate of the Women's Liberation movement followed the general pattern for the New Left of the 1960s.

Many of us, after more than ten long years of experience in a series of movements, and especially the Women's Liberation movement, have become Marxist-Leninists – not because we read books, but because we fought and lost too many battles, then read the books. In short, we must begin again. This time, however, we are far better armed, in terms of ideology and practice, not to repeat the mistakes of the past, not to compromise with counterrevolutionary racism and sexism, not to be sucked into petty bourgeois class collaborationism, not to fail in our struggle to build an organization, a fighting organization for the liberation of our sisters, our brothers, ourselves.

NOTES

1. Barbara Dudley, "Report on the Conference," Socialist Revolution (October-December 1975), pp. 109, 111, 114.
2. Ibid., pp. 111, 114.
3. Barbara Ehrenreich, "Speech by Barbara Ehrenreich," Socialist Revolution (October-December 1975), p. 89.
4. Dudley, p. 107.

The Sisterhood Ripoff:

The Destruction of the Left in the Professional Women's Caucuses

While specifically concerned with women's caucuses, the following article is applicable to any progressive movement within the petty bourgeoisie.

In Canada we have learned to our sorrow that the Canadian government has proved an apt pupils of its "big brother" in the United States when it comes to the theory and practice of co-optation coupled with judicious repression. Both the Canadian student movement and the Canadian women's movement have suffered because the Canadian government, while two steps behind the USA, was at the same time two steps ahead of progressive forces in Canada. Indeed, no sooner had the Canadian women's movement gathered its forces than the government began its program to drown the movement in mountains of paper and oceans of verbiage. Of course, the devastation of entire forests to produce paper full of worthless promises and pious

Address given as part of the Women's Studies in Sociology colloquium series, York University, March 13, 1975, Downsview, Ontario and published in the Bulletin of Women in Canadian Sociology *(Femmes et Sociologie Canadienne), Vol. 11, No. 2, April, 1975.*

intentions has resulted in not one significant improvement for women. However, if the government can use the United States as a school of what to do to assure that no significant change ever occurs, it follows that progressive forces in Canada can also learn from the United States – and most often can learn from the U.S. left what not to do. In the interests of learning what not to do we shall concern ourselves with a generalized scenario of the repression of the left in professional women's associations as it was played out in the United States.

Women's caucuses in professional associations within the United States began as part of the agitation for radical and critical social science. Many of the women involved in radical and critical social science were also part of Women's Liberation – when it was still a radical movement. In the course of calling for special sessions and meetings on the issues of critical social science, meetings to discuss the institutionalized discrimination against women in universities and colleges were also called. Thus, the original women's caucuses were in most cases part and parcel of the radical student movement represented by graduate students and junior faculty. The early caucuses were characterized by the militance, impudence, and radical calls for change that were characteristic of the rebellious mood of the late sixties. For this reason, "respectable" and highly professionalized career women shunned the radical caucuses, often condemning them openly in order to assure the men who controlled their professional careers that they were loyal women who wanted no part of these "uncouth" and unwashed heretical goings-on.

However, as the women's liberation movement gained momentum and the issue of discrimination against women gained legitimacy, the attitude of professionalized women changed. Once it was relatively "safe" to approach the issue of injustice towards women it also became apparent to these women that distinct advantages and economic improvements might be gained through their espousal of "equal opportunity" for women. Professionalized women (genuine "career" women) began to attend caucus meetings. The result was a two-line struggle that rapidly emerged within the caucuses. (At this point we shall confine ourselves to sociology, with the proviso that the scenario in sociology was quite typical of the general process that unfolded in most other disciplines.)

We may term the two lines as Careerist and Radical. The Careerist line was essentially a call for economism, that is, to limit agitation and demands to career and salary issues or "equal opportunity." The economist line of the Careerists implicitly called for strategies to limit competition with men (usually by staking out exclusively female programs and topics) and the rejection of programs that went beyond minimal reformism. Calls to combat discrimination were coupled with a heavy ideological emphasis upon "sisterhood." In this context, "sisterhood" functioned very much like nationalism does for a national minority: that is, this appeal called for the unity of women essentially as a "status group," in the sense that all women had womantude in common. The result of the "status group" approach was to blur class lines and real conflict of interest and ideology – with disastrous results for the left, as we shall see.

The Radicals were actually a much more heterogeneous group than the Careerists. While the Careerists had career ambitions as the real basis of their unity, the Radicals had little in common except militance. Perhaps the principal dividing line within the Radical group was between radical feminists (men are the principal enemy) and socialists (capitalism is the principal enemy). What the Radicals had in common, despite their ideological disunity, was a genuinely radical (as opposed to reformist) call for cultural and social transformation of society as essential to the liberation of women. They called for democratization; they opposed the professional hierarchy; they behaved with consistent bad taste toward the professional mandarins; they called for revolutionary women's studies programs; they wore their hair long and often did not bother with brassieres.

The conflict between the Radicals and Careerists led to acrimony and stalemated meetings. At the same time, the antics of the Radicals were a constant threat to the image of the Careerists who feared being identified with the radical activists. Attempts to use "sisterhood" as a means to get the Radicals to change their ways and accept leadership from the Careerists were met with denunciations of "elitism" (from the radical feminists) and "reactionary" (from the socialists).

The failure of the Careerists to establish control over the original radical women's caucuses led them to form their own organization, Sociologists for Women in Society (SWS). The formation of the careerist SWS spelled the defeat of the left and the formulation of the oppression of women in purely economist and reformist terms.

The formation of the SWS along liberal-reformist lines opened up communication with the professional oligarchy.

Indeed, the corporate-liberal oligarchs were eager to deal with the Careerists as a means of containing the radical threat posed by the earlier women's caucuses (and their repellent connections with the radical student movement). The Careerists were the sort of people the oligarchs could deal with: "reasonable" reformers amenable to "rational debate." In other words, the professional oligarchs could feel confident that the Careerists would settle for minor concessions, relatively meaningless reforms, pious declarations of support and other cheap variations on tokenism, delay and the avoidance of any significant change. In short, the "rational" and "reasonable" Careerists were manageable.

The "recognition" and minor concessions granted to the SWS were touted as proof that liberal-reformist and decorous academic styles were superior strategically, that they "produced results." This undercut the position of the Radicals, who could be charged with "irresponsibility" and unwitting sabotage with their uncouth manners and "unrealistic" demands. With the Radicals frozen out by the collusion between SWS and the male-dominated professional leadership it became possible to define women's agitation along strictly professional and reformist lines.

The scenario played out in the profession also took place within individual colleges and universities, particularly around women's studies programs. Usually women's studies programs arose as a demand of Women's Liberation as the women's arm of the student movement for democratization and reform of the university. Where that was the case, the woman students fighting for women's studies wished for an organization, curriculum and staff that reflected the progressive demands of the student movement. Early women's studies programs tended to bring in staff who were progressive; this in turn alarmed university and college administrations. The result was a dual tactic of financial strangulation and staff purges until a highly professional staff could replace the progressives and a professional curriculum and organization could replace the early innovating programs. Careerists were as eager for this event as were university administrations because women's studies under Careerist control provided an area free from male competition. A Careerist could pursue mainstream social science so long as it touched in some way upon "women" (as if women were bizarre creatures who could be studied in isolation). Women's studies thus became a "secure base area" for female careerists, offering jobs, promotions, salaries, forms of special recognition – all blissfully secured from male control and competition. Equally, the radical women's liberationists who posed a threat to professional careerism were also safely driven out of the Careerists' new compound. The fact that these very same Radicals had taken the risks, fought the battles, and organized the movement which the Careerists now so eagerly exploited became a forbidden topic. The Careerists pretended that the "man-hating crazies" and the "wild-eyed radicals" had simply been an impediment to the progress of professional women. What bitterness it still invokes! Professionalized career women who had virulently attacked the early agitation now flocking greedily to devour the spoils and destroy the women who had set the table and spread the feast!*

The purely economist and reformist programs and policies of organizations like SWS stripped women's agitation within the professions of its radical content. Women's studies in most cases became nothing more than a special subject area limited to liberal-professional styles of work. The imposition of professional hiring criteria and professional hierarchical structures served to assure that women's studies programs would present no threat to the dominant corporate-liberal professional hegemony. Women's studies was in this manner reduced to reflect the general bankruptcy that professional liberalism produced in the social sciences. If corporate liberalism represented failure in analysis, intellectual content and policy implications for the poor, for national minorities, for the American working class, could it be expected to serve the intellectual needs of women's liberation? The triumph of professionalism was the defeat of the intellectual and theoretical development essential to the generation of adequate analysis of the oppression and exploitation of women. The threat was indeed contained.

---

* The author, it should go without saying, is not referring to those women who have consistently stood for genuine women's studies and other progressive action to ameliorate the devastating effects of institutionalized discrimination against women. The tone of revulsion is directed at those opportunists who have purged, betrayed, and hopped on the bandwagon purely in their own career interests and whose programs, organizations and actions are antagonistic to the real needs of women in education. After all, we did not organize Women's Liberation to maximize the career opportunities of reactionaries and flunkies.

The rise of SWS and the co-optation of women's studies was part of the general purge that was being carried out against radicals and radical activists in North American universities and colleges. The professionalized Careerists' "sisterhood" song suddenly evaporated when the opportunity to purge the radical opposition presented itself. Women who had built careers in the context of liberal professionalism were as hostile to the intellectual and social challenge of the radicals as were their male counterparts. Sisterhood had progressed from bad joke to obscenity.

We have presented a generalized and abstracted analysis, not a specific history. We can now note that there is a typical sequence to the scenario of repression and co-optation, a scenario that was enacted not only in women's caucuses, but in many radical caucuses as well. The virtue of the history of women's organizations is the clarity with which the entire play unfolds:

Scene I: Left progressive youth (graduate students, junior faculty) begin agitation by raising radical critiques, demanding potentially radical changes, documenting injustices, engaging in direct actions until such time as they are perceived as a real threat by the professional Establishment.

Scene II: Left progressives have created a real threat and achieved some degree of legitimacy around issues of discrimination and injustice. The liberal progressives hop on the bandwagon to form a Center. The Center provides an alternative to the Left and provides respectability. With respectability the more conservative Careerists are willing to join the Center, but only if the Left can be purged or operatively divorced from the "respectables."

Scene III: The Center (progressive liberals) and Right (conservative careerists) form a separate organization. The organization solves the problem of control by organizing itself along professional-hierarchical lines (cf. the many critiques of "elitism" being raised against the SWS). The Left may join (as rank and file) the Center-Right Coalition organization, but its undemocratic structure and behind-the-scenes decision-making assures that the Left will remain an impotent opposition, no more than a general annoyance at plenary meetings.

Scene IV: With the Center-Right Coalition firmly in control of the new organization, the redefinition of "women's struggle" is effectively – and publicly – carried through. "Equal opportunity" and a respectable-professional image dominate the organization. It is now possible for the leadership of the Center-Right organization to carry out an attack against the legitimacy of the original Left progressive agitators. The Left progressives are presented as unprofessional, inccmpetent, irresponsible. The attack escalates. The Left progressives are not only unprofessional, incompetent and irresponsible, they are also communists, disruptors, man-haters, lesbians, dominating male-identified castrating maniacs. The result of these assaults is to provoke the Left progressives (those who have been foolish enough even to remain in such an organization) to shrill defense and counter-denunciation. The outcome is the increasing isolation of the Left progressives.

Scene V: The Center-Right Coalition organization is acceptable to the professional (male-dominated) Establishment and to university administrations. It is even happily embraced by federal agencies and funding sources. The Left progressives are frozen out and starved for funds and recognition. The stage is now set for co-optation, as negotiations are undertaken between the Establishment and the Center-Right organization.

Scene VI: The result of the negotiations between the Center-Right organization and the professional Establishment are a series of co-optive minor concessions and token representation covered by a great deal of hypocritical liberal-high-flown verbiage about "justice" and "equal opportunity" and "equality." Close analysis will show that most of the concessions are in fact career rewards to the leadership of the Center-Right organization – the pay-off for their effective containment of the "radical threat." These concessions are paraded as "successes" and touted as signs of better things yet to come under the leadership of the Center-Right organization. These "victories" serve to validate the Center-Right leadership for the trusting rank and file (who are in most cases sincere liberals which, by definition, means that they are completely incompetent politicians). As a result, the remnants of the Left still hanging-in are further discredited. The Center-Right leadership is now able to argue that the Left progressives actually jeopardize the hopes of "equal opportunity" gains which the Center-Right leadership promises will result from their ability to negotiate (reason together with) the professional Establishment.

<u>Scene VII</u>: The Left is by now completely defeated. However, the Center has gone down with the Left. The legitimacy of the Center rested upon their role as an "alternative" to the radical threat. During the period of respectability and negotiation (Scenes III to VI) the Establishment, university administrations and government agencies have been busily promoting the right-wing of the organization into pay-off positions of influence and prestige. This undermines the progressive liberal Center. With the purging of the Left, the Right no longer <u>needs</u> the Center, which now shifts into opposition. The Center, which participated in the destruction of the Left, now becomes, operatively, THE Left. After a road of betrayal and self-promotion, the "virtuous" Center now assumes the martyrdom of Truth, Goodness and Beauty.

<u>Scene VIII</u>: We have now arrived at the present. Equal opportunity for women is respectable. The radical threat is contained. The Right leadership keeps it contained – for like George Meany, if they cannot keep the troops in line they will lose their pay-offs. The rank and file withers away in a state of apathy and general disillusion – although like all liberals, they cannot understand what happened and why the fine days of sisterhood have passed away. Corporate-liberal professional hegemony is safe from radical and from female attack. The "professional reformers" carry out "negotiations" with various interested Establishments and occasionally bother to report "progress" and make "promises" to a listless rank and file. The professional association, the profession, the university administration remain oppressive and male-dominated, studded with a black or female token here and there. <u>Nothing has changed</u>. "Reformism" has triumphed again. Paternalism is replaced by maternalism and the Republic and the Profession are safe from the unwashed masses.

One must point out that the defeat of the Left – which was never marked by political or ideological coherence – has been greatly facilitated by both the illusions of "sisterhood" and "radical feminist" politics. The ideology of sisterhood in many cases was successfully manipulated to contain real criticism or a real challenge to the political manueverings of the Center-Right Coalition. The self-interested careerist motivations of these women were effectively blurred by the assumption of unity and sisterhood. Sisterhood combined with the radical feminist phobia against men-in-general led the non-socialist Left into alliances with the Center (often together against the "male-dominated" female Left). The irony, of course, is that the simple-minded politics of the radical feminists made them easy prey to the Center-Right coalition that was in fact selling out the real interests of   - women in return for rewards from the male-dominated Establishment! The radical feminists made it easy for the Center-Right coalition to claim the ability to control the "radicals" — and the ability to control the radicals was the only bargaining power that the Center-Right reformist coalition had! Their pay-offs were dependent upon their perceived ability to "keep the women in line."

Such is the sorry history of the radical women's caucuses. We are left without real gains for the equality of women. We are left without an intellectual enterprise capable truly of analyzing the oppression and exploitation of women. We are left without a Left — the universities and women are back in 1952. The lessons are certainly clear: liberalism and reformism hold out no hope to women, nor any hope to any oppressed and exploited sector of North American society. The only way that the repetition of the co-optive scenario can be broken is through the development of both political sophistication and theoretical adequacy. This requires that the Left be a genuine Left — that it be organized, that it be founded on a basis of ideological, analytical and organizational unity. The purge of the U.S. universities has been so devastating that it is unlikely that recovery is possible in the near future. Canada may yet remain in question. Let us hope Canada may be saved from the dismal scenario of betrayal and self-interest that devastated the United States.